# Advance Praise for *People Habitat*

"Kaid Benfield distills the true essence of a broad range of city-building and sustainability issues more often and more capably than almost anyone else I've ever read. Many authors write because they're hoping to change things for the better, and it's easy to explode into shouting and fist-pounding when all is not well in the world. Kaid, however, keeps it positive better than anyone else I read, repeatedly pointing out places and principles done well, and higher ideals to which we should aspire."

—Stephen A. Mouzon,
author, *The Original Green: Unlocking the Mystery of True Sustainability*

ᕱᕲ

"I strongly encourage anyone with even a passing interest in the quality of the place where they live to read Kaid Benfield's writing. His framing of the ecology of 'people habitat' is immensely useful in celebrating how an enormous number of small actions to create healthier local places can contribute to a healthier planet."

—Keith Laughlin,
President, Rails-to-Trails Conservancy

ᕱᕲ

"Environmentalist Kaid Benfield clearly explains how dense cities, if done right, are a friend not an enemy of nature. I always have my students read a blog or two of his on walkable, mixed use, transit-rich, livable, healthy, and lovable urbanism. *People Habitat* finally gathers his insightful writings into its own dense little city of ideas."

—Douglas Kelbaugh,
Professor and Dean Emeritus of Architecture and Urban Planning,
University of Michigan

ᕱᕲ

"Kaid Benfield, like Jane Jacobs, is a talented writer who isn't burdened by preconceptions or jargon, who can explain the ideas of others or express his own in a style that is accessible and comprehensible. These 25 essays are not just about cities; they are about making sense of the way we live."

—Lloyd Alter,
Managing Editor, *Treehugger.com*

D1232169

# PEOPLE HABITAT

## 25 Ways to Think About Greener, Healthier Cities

Essays by F. Kaid Benfield

People Habitat Communications ■ 2014

# Table of Contents

# Acknowledgments

This book would have suffered greatly but for the intellect and diligence of its principal editor, Meghan Bogaerts, and the talent, professionalism, and good spirits of its principal designer, Brenda Ruby. Both were and are a delight to work with and very good at their tasks. It also would not be the same without my frequent writing collaborator, Lee Epstein, co-author of two of these essays and someone whose friendship and insights contribute to my thinking and writing even when he isn't trying to. Thank you, Meghan, Brenda, and Lee.

Special thanks also to the excellent photographers and illustrators who have allowed their work to enhance this book through commercial use license and personal communications. To be honest, I'm not sure I would have wanted to write it without your generosity and kindness.

The life of a writer can be a lonely one at times, punctuated by episodes of doubt. Thanks so much to those who have supported and encouraged my writing on these topics. You keep me going. I have to begin with Phil Gutis, former communications director at the Natural Resources Defense Council who always believed in my instincts, and Ian Wilker, without whom there never would have been the blog from which most of these essays were born. Lloyd Alter, Richard Florida, and David Whitaker, you are too kind in encouraging my work, but I am honored by your good words along the way. I also have drawn confidence and energy from the folks at *The Atlantic*, *The Atlantic Cities*, and *The Sustainable Cities Collective*, whom I cannot thank enough for recruiting me and publishing my articles.

The list of fellow travelers in the quest for better cities whose immense talent and dedication inspires me daily is long, but it must begin with my direct collaborators in my daily professional life, including Eliot Allen, Jessica Millman, Marissa Ramirez, David Dixon, and my colleague and longtime sister-in-arms Shelley Poticha.

I also must thank those at NRDC past and present for their impact on my career and thus on this book. I might never have begun the journey for better cities at all without the example of my friend David Goldstein, and these topics were informed by five years of daily conversations with Rachel Sohmer. It was NRDC's presidents John Adams and Frances Beinecke, however, who gave me the trust and professional room to pursue a new kind of environmentalism under our organization's flag. The ideas that culminated in this book would not have happened without your support and, I must admit, indulgence. Ashok Gupta, you have understood and supported my pursuit of these ideas more than anyone, and in the process have become a great friend. To all of NRDC's many friends and supporters, I cannot thank you enough for enabling our organization to become as strong and effective as it has.

I have always reached outside my employer for ideas, learning, and formal and informal partnerships, every one of which has informed this book. This has led me to a very special friendship and professional relationship with Don Chen, the best big-picture thinker I know, and to so many mentors in the wonderful world of green urbanism. I can't possibly name all, but I can't imagine a page such as this without acknowledging the influence and friendship of Victor Dover, John Norquist, Steve Mouzon, Reid Ewing, Jane LaFleur, Hank Dittmar, Chuck Wolfe, Peter Calthorpe, Chuck Marohn, and David Crossley.

Finally, I have reserved the most special thanks for Sharon Marsh. I would adore you even without your incredible intellect, insight, and professional judgment, all of which made this a better book. But those qualities and many more make you my most trusted partner of all.

# Prologue:

## Cities of the Imagination

New York City *(photo by F. Kaid Benfield)*

As children, we spend a lot of time imagining things we haven't experienced yet, and imagining unknown parts of things we have begun to experience. That's the way it was for me and cities as a kid.

This book was born from my imagined impressions of cities before I actually experienced them, from my measure of cities against that imagination, and from my imagination yet again, as I consider how real cities might reach our best aspirations for them as habitat for people. It is the fourth book about some aspect of cities with my name on the cover.

I am excited about it: It is the one truest to my heart and was the most fun to write. Unlike the others, each of which pursued a singular topic in depth and explored points of advocacy on behalf of my employers, this one comes from me alone. I intend it to be broad in its reach, exploring many issues related by no more of a central premise than asking readers to think with me about how to make human settlement as good as possible. That may sound a bit glib, but I hope to persuade you to join me in considering some of the more difficult issues, the ones where the answers aren't so clear.

I owe the title *People Habitat* to my friend Trisha White, an expert on the interactions between the built environment and wildlife. Trisha believes wildlife does best when nature's critters have a realm that is primarily their own, and when we humans have the same—a "people habitat" distinct from places where wildlife is primary and we are secondary. I thought Trisha captured a lot in that simple phrase, which I first heard at a meeting and never forgot.

People "habitat" may borrow a word from the field of wildlife ecology but it evokes a different sort of ecology, one centered on humans. Nature works best when it is in balance, and that leads me to a guiding principle: like the natural environment when operating at its best, the built environment created by us humans should achieve harmony among its various parts and with the larger world upon which it depends. A second guiding principle is that, while the ecology of the natural world concerns itself primarily with the interdependence of species and the health of ecosystems, the ecology of people habitat concerns itself also with our relationships as humans to each other, and with the health of communities that support those relationships and allow us to flourish.

Thinking spatially, wildlife habitat may be conceived as a realm that starts in a nest or den and extends outward from there. People habitat is similar: our domain begins in our homes but also extends outward, to our neighborhoods, our cities or towns, and even to the regions beyond, which I discuss in the first chapter. I believe we humans have an opportunity and a duty to make our habitat work both for us as people and for the sustainable health of the planet writ large.

For most of us, our experience of the human environment—our own people habitat, if you will—begins as children, as we discover the things around us. My friend Chuck Wolfe, for example, wrote a terrific essay called "Rediscovering the Urban Eye of a Child," which was published on his blog *myurbanist* (and, under a different title, on the website of *The Atlantic*).

Udine, Italy *(photo courtesy of Chuck Wolfe)*

An astute observer of cities and a gifted photographer, Chuck traces his roots for both, recalling trips as a child to cities abroad with his father, an urban planning professor. He shares a number of photos he took as a 12-year-old in and around Mediterranean cities. If the colors have lost some oomph over the years, those photos remain well-composed and, as Chuck writes, reflective even then of the urbanist attributes he values today such as public spaces, walkable streets, and the textures of historic architecture.

Knowing Chuck, I wasn't surprised to learn from his writing that he was a precocious and observant child; but I was struck by his assimilation of urban wisdom from his father at that age. I had a very different background.

In particular, as a kid living with working-class parents in a small, sleepy southern city, I mostly *imagined*—rather than experienced— larger American cities of consequence, or historic cities abroad. I was in my late 30s before I could afford a trip out of the country, and I am quite sure I did not even know there was such a thing as urban planning until almost as late in life. My parents had tons of smarts and great instincts, but no higher education, and I was pretty much on my own for finding my way into college, then law school, and eventually a profession. I made it up as I went along. I still am.

My hometown of Asheville, North Carolina was hardly without its merits, most of all its location smack in the middle of the majestic southern Appalachian Mountains, with the Blue Ridge to the northeast and the Great Smokies to the southwest. We could get to a mountaintop picnic area or trail faster than I can now get to work, and I loved it (while taking my unique natural surroundings for granted, of course, as kids are wont to do). When not exploring nature, chances are I was playing tennis, teaching myself guitar, or spending time with various church youth groups, because that's what many of us did in that time and place.

We did have a smallish downtown, though, and instinctively that's where I wanted to be on a Saturday, if I wasn't doing one of those other things. When I was around the age when Chuck took his photos, I would hop on the city bus, take myself downtown, and hang out. I loved the city library, the tiny downtown park and larger main square, the Woolworth's, the movie theater, the music store. Especially the library and music store. Downtown, sleepy though it was, seemed like a place where things happened, where grownups more important than I did...what, exactly? If I considered that part at all, it was with my imagination.

I suppose that, most of all, downtown Asheville was a place with some liveliness: people shopping, selling, eating out, going to movies, or whatever. As a *de facto* only child (I wasn't, technically, but that's perhaps a story for a different kind of book) of two working parents, I was alone a lot of the time, well before the phrase "latch-key kid" entered the lexicon; hanging out in a place with a bit of life mitigated that problem.

Asheville *(photo courtesy of Jane 023)*

So, in my own way, I had stumbled upon some of the amenities that even small-city downtowns, if they are good ones, can provide: animation; a variety of activities close at hand; the possibility of a chance encounter with a friend or interesting stranger. Asheville also had, and still has, lovely residential neighborhoods—many with spectacular views, because the city contains real (if small) mountains within its borders. But I went to the residential areas to see friends or attend planned events; I didn't go just to go, as I did with respect to downtown.

(Some readers may now know Asheville as a popular destination town of character and creativity—as it was once before, around the turn of the 20th century and a couple of decades thereafter. But I grew up there in between its heydays. Church socials were where it was at.)

My forays into our city center notwithstanding, "real" cities were things I saw on TV, or occasionally heard about from distant relatives who, for reasons still not clear to me, actually lived in Manhattan. In my mind, New York City was very tall, exotic buildings and lots of stores and bright lights. A subway! Los Angeles was Disneyland, the beach, cool-looking freeways, and Hollywood. Cleveland was a place with a baseball team whose games came in late at night on a clear-channel radio station.

These imagined places were about as far from my everyday reality as one can imagine, which may be why I was drawn to them
so strongly (in addition to the fact that all the people on TV who
supposedly lived in them seemed so cool). I now have friends and
colleagues who actually grew up in New York City and, honestly, I
have a hard time conjuring what it was like for them, since to me real
cities were for grownups, not kids.

I did have two immensely important, in-person childhood experiences of big cities. When I was a preteen, I took a trip to Los Angeles to visit my half-brother. I actually went alone, changing planes
in Atlanta, with the airline alerted to look after me. Alex and his wife
met me at what is now LAX airport.

Vintage postcard, Los Angeles *(Public Domain)*

It was pretty awesome at that age, being away from my parents,
and especially seeing Disneyland and the freeways, along with taking
a moonlit horseback ride that seems unfathomable anywhere near today's LA. Later that summer—or was it the next?—my mother took
me to New York City to visit different relatives. It was an all-night
bus ride to Washington, DC, where we changed to the train for New
York. All the tourist sites were exciting and, being the nerdy kid that
I was, I wanted to see the United Nations. I still have a little blue UN

flag from that trip. These short visits provided still more material for my budding urban imagination.

And my urban imagination remained just that; there were no more big cities for me until I went off to college in Atlanta. In fact, one can understand my life's quest, in a way, as a journey seeking to attain those cities of my child's imagination. I always had a sense that cities were my true home, where I felt most comfortable on an everyday basis. But that didn't necessarily make them less elusive: The great American writer Thomas Wolfe, an Asheville native, memorably wrote, "You can't go home again." Indeed you can't, especially if "home" was an experience linked as much to places imagined as to those that were real.

But that hasn't kept me from trying.

When in Atlanta, I soaked up everything the city had to offer that I could afford, and quite a few things that I couldn't, now that I think about it. Atlanta had a lot going on in those days, making its transition from a sleepier place to an exciting one where businesses boomed and people flocked; this was long before downtown was largely abandoned and the whole place choked to death by suburban sprawl and gridlocked traffic. It was a great time to be there. Next came Washington, DC for law school, which actually wasn't so great in those post-riot years (parts of the city were burned in 1968); but I stayed, and over time I have watched Washington become the great international city that it now is. And through travel I've now experienced many more cities.

All along the way, I've been picking up bits of information and clues about what makes cities great. I've never had any formal training in that, and didn't have any professional connection to these issues, either, until late in my career. I'm basically a self-taught urbanist.

To bring this piece of writing back home, I'm still making my own way, really, just as I did as a kid in the South over four decades ago. I learned not from my forebears and childhood urban experiences, as my friend Chuck did, but from my curiosity, and from a sense that life (and place) could be better. I suspect that many readers are on that same quest to make cities better.

To that end, I am sharing 25 essays related to points I believe are useful to consider as we enjoy and improve this wondrous invention that we call "cities." It is less expository writing than storytelling, more illustration than proclamation. While I will always say exactly what I think—or believe I am learning—about these subjects, polemic writing and thinking don't interest me. The nooks and crannies do.

I will also present some discussion of particular places or supplementary bits of information that add related ideas to the principal essay themes. It was difficult to choose just 25 subjects, but the choices were not arbitrary. By intention, these ideas are not all in line with prevailing environmental and urbanist thinking, not all fully formed and, truth be told, not all fully consistent with each other. I believe that's as it should be. We live in a world of questions as much as answers; anyone who pretends to have all the answers is faking it, in my humble opinion.

I should also add that I make no claim that my 25 subjects are the 25 most objectively important, though I hope you will agree that some of them belong in that group. Rather, they are subjects on which I feel I have something to share, something I have discovered that interests me and that I hope will interest you.

To me the notions in these 25 essays include salient ones, challenging ones, and a couple that are just fun. They can be read in any order you like. They are the stories I most wanted to share, and I hope you enjoy reading them as much as I enjoyed writing them.

## More about This Book

In 2007, Ian Wilker, my then colleague at the Natural Resources Defense Council, recruited me for a new blog, to be called *Switchboard*, he was starting at the organization. Knowing my love of writing and reflection, Ian thought I would be a natural. Several years and well over a thousand blog posts later, I suppose he has been proven right. I have been flattered that my articles have proven popular with readers, and flattered further that several other websites now publish my work regularly. I didn't begin with that ambition; I just had things I wanted to say, discoveries I wanted to share, questions I wanted to raise. Ian's site became my medium, and I still haven't run out of ideas for it.

Many of the essays and themes in *People Habitat* were born on *Switchboard*. A thousand-plus pieces of writing have given me a lot of raw material and quite a chance to consider and refine ideas about the places where we live, work, and play. A reader of my blog will recognize some of the subject matter, brought up to date and in many cases combined and expanded in what I hope are fresh ways.

Regulars may also recognize in the writing some of my architect, planner, and environmental friends, from whom I am constantly learning and whose ideas I mention often. I love sharing their insights. In borrowing from the blog, I attempted to choose topics with lasting resonance.

(It is important to distinguish my work on this book with that of my principal employer. Throughout the period during which I wrote this book, I was employed by the Natural Resources Defense Council in its Washington, DC office. NRDC is a nonprofit environmental advocacy organization with its headquarters in New York City and offices in Washington, San Francisco, Los Angeles, Chicago, and Beijing. I wrote the book on my own time, however; NRDC's staff and resources were not involved in its concept or review in any way. The opinions expressed in the book are mine and mine alone.)

# 1.

# It's Not Really about Cities

Palo Alto City Limit *(photo courtesy of Martin Jambon)*

Allow me to be deliberatively provocative: although this is a book about cities, in some senses "cities" don't matter nearly as much as we sometimes suggest. To the environment and the economy, neighborhoods and metropolitan regions matter more.

Legally, cities are municipalities with strictly drawn formal boundaries—but that is not how most people use the word. And that's where we can get into trouble when it comes to understanding them. I prefer to think in terms of metropolitan regions, which provide the economic and environmental scale of people habitat, and neighborhoods, which provide the human scale.

Let me give an example of how language about cities can be confusing: a couple of years ago, a professional friend returned from a meeting in which there was discussion about so-called "shrinking cities." This is a very sharp, aware guy. At that meeting someone reportedly said that "29 US cities have grown recently and the rest have shrunk." My friend wondered if we should refocus the field of smart growth (oversimplified, an ethos encouraging compact development patterns supported by walkability and transit) away from being about "growth," since so few places are actually growing.

That didn't sound right to me at all, so I checked the facts: There were 366 metropolitan areas tracked by the US government as of 2010; cumulatively, they *grew* by 10.8 percent in between 2000 and 2010. Of the 50 largest, 45 grew and only 5 declined in population during that decade. One of the five, New Orleans, is a special case because of the effects of Hurricane Katrina in 2005; two of the five grew population in their suburban areas, even while declining overall. Other than New Orleans, only Buffalo and Pittsburgh declined in population in both their core cities and their suburbs between 2000 and 2010. Overall, that's a lot of growth, and nearly all US metros—even the ones that have lost population—have expanded their spatial footprint, the amount of land that they occupy. That's not shrinking.

Each US "metropolitan statistical area," as defined by the US Office of Management and Budget, has one or more "core cities," generally the older, centrally located municipality for which the metro area is informally known (for example, Washington, DC is a core city for the Washington MSA). Unfortunately, the population of these inner, core cities was in decline just about everywhere in America during the second half of the 20th century as population and investment flew to the suburbs. Municipal Washington, where I live, lost an astounding 29 percent of its population between 1950 and 2000.

But growth didn't stop; it just shifted beyond the core cities. Recently, even that trend is reversing, faster in some places than others. So why did my statistics vary so drastically from those of the speaker at my friend's meeting?

My guess is that the speaker had a point he or she wanted to make and chose a select set of facts to support it—probably looking only at a subset of the places tracked by the census, and probably looking only at what was happening inside the jurisdictional boundaries of the older cities located in the centers of their expanding metro regions.

Atlanta city limits superimposed on satellite photo of metro Atlanta
(*via Google Earth*)

Those jurisdictional city boundaries—the "city limits"—are largely arbitrary in today's world. They date back to the early 20th or even 19th century in many cases, are frequently drawn in crazy ways, and bear little relation to how places function now. Consider the image in this chapter that shows the city limits of Atlanta drawn on a satellite photo of what is now the real Atlanta.

Whatever the origin of the statement about shrinking cities, the resulting impression—that few places are growing—could not be more false. It misled my friend and it could mislead policy-makers into some very ill-informed decisions. Here's how the problem occurs: Merriam-Webster defines a city as "an inhabited place of greater size, population, or importance than a town or village." That's the way most of us use the word, most of the time.

But Merriam-Webster also defines a city as "a usually large or important municipality in the United States governed under a charter granted by the state." These are two overlapping but very different things: using the first definition, one might say that "Atlanta" is a sprawling metropolis and powerful economic entity with a population of over 5.4 million people; but, using the second, Atlanta becomes a much smaller area containing only 432,000 residents (as of 2011). Metropolitan Atlanta holds over twelve times the population of the "city" of Atlanta.

In other words, the smaller, jurisdictional Atlanta may mean something to candidates for city office and cartographers, but it has very little to do with economic or environmental reality. Let's zoom in. See the neighborhood-scaled satellite image with the bright, zigzagging line? That line marks a portion of the city limits of Atlanta. If there is a meaningful distinction in the real world to be made between the areas inside and outside the official city boundary, it sure eludes me.

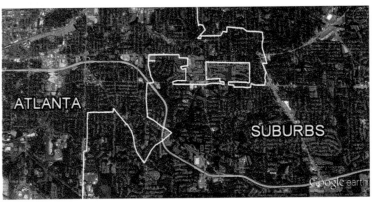

Boundary between city of Atlanta and it suburbs
(*satellite image by USGS, via Google Earth*)

As the Brookings Institution puts it, *metropolitan regions* "are our hubs of research and innovation, our centers of human capital, and our gateways of trade and immigration. They are, in short, the drivers of our economy, and American competitiveness depends on their vitality."

As put by one Barack Obama during his first presidential campaign:

"That is the new metropolitan reality and we need a
new strategy that reflects it—a strategy that's about
South Florida as much as Miami; that's about Mesa and
Scottsdale as much as Phoenix; that's about Stamford and
Northern New Jersey as much as New York City."

How about another example? My wife and I live in the city of Washington, DC, but she works in nearby suburban Virginia; I ride my bike pretty much every weekend from my house into Maryland and back without even noticing where the jurisdictional boundary is. Sometimes I return home along a street where the houses on the left side are in the District of Columbia and those on the right are in Maryland.

I'm not exactly sure whether my doctor's office is in DC or Maryland. I just know it's close to the boundary; the street and buildings look exactly the same on both sides. My colleagues at the office go home in the evenings to a dozen different municipalities.

Environmental media don't respect political boundaries, either: The Potomac and Anacostia Rivers receive runoff from Virginia and Maryland as well as from the jurisdictional cities of Washington and Alexandria; the Chesapeake Bay watershed includes parts of seven states and scores of municipalities. The air in Chicago moves freely around the seven counties and 284 separate municipalities just within the Illinois part of the region, to say nothing of those in nearby Wisconsin and Indiana. Very little of the energy consumed within the jurisdictional limits of the city of San Francisco is generated there. And so on. Statistics about only what is happening inside city limits seldom tell us much about what is relevant environmentally.

I would submit that the other scale (besides metropolitan regions) of people habitat that matters the most to the greatest number of people is the neighborhood. Neighborhoods are where we eat and sleep and where, if we are lucky, our kids play and go to school; where we shop for food, take our dry cleaning, and maybe grab a bite to eat; where we meet neighbors on the street or in community gatherings;

if we're really lucky, the neighborhood will even have a library branch and a hardware store.

While those of us who live in metropolitan areas—and that includes 83 percent of all Americans—zip all around them to visit friends, conduct business, and shop, we're usually going to other neighborhoods when we do. If the region represents the economic scale of real cities, the neighborhood represents the human scale.

Barcelona *(photo by F. Kaid Benfield)*

Neighborhoods are also the scale at which land development takes place, where new buildings and facilities are proposed, debated, and constructed. They are where development decisions actually occur, and where we must pay attention if we want to have influence. In fact, one of the best ways to reduce the environmental footprint of a region is to revitalize older neighborhoods that have lost population, because their relatively central locations reduce transportation emissions and they require little if any increase in runoff-causing impervious surface. They also help conserve land by obviating additional increments of suburban sprawl.

So where does that leave cities in the jurisdictional sense of the word? They certainly remain very important politically. In big cities, we can address problems at scale when we lack the legal and regulatory tools to do so regionally. Municipalities are where we frequently advocate stormwater regulation, building standards, complete streets, zoning reform, and even climate policy. It's where we can get things accomplished.

But that's partly because cities are the low-hanging fruit of environmental standards and regulation. We often look to mayors, for example, for leadership on environmental issues, even though in the case of big cities their authority is limited to the parts of their regions that are almost always the most sustainable already, on a per capita basis. It frequently pays off: urban mayors tend to be more innovative and progressive than their suburban counterparts.

But, when we focus inside the city limits instead of on the region, we're missing much of the problem, and we shouldn't pretend otherwise. Stormwater runoff per capita is typically much higher in sprawling suburbs, as are emissions of all sorts, particularly those related to transportation.

One can even make the case that regulators should be going easier on relatively compactly settled core cities and neighborhoods than on sprawling places: to paraphrase David Owen, author of the book *Green Metropolis*, why put skinny people on diets? My personal view is that our framework of environmental regulation absolutely should be tougher on sprawling places than urban ones, but that urban ones should also do their fair share to heal our ecosystems, through appropriate standards, safeguards, and mitigation.

Unfortunately, I think we remain relatively less attentive to the suburbs, largely because our crazy patchwork of suburban municipalities makes them legally so diffuse; with very rare exceptions, there simply is no regional authority to address the metropolis as a whole. Addressing municipalities one by one, even if we had the resources to do so, can lead to perverse results, since sometimes the most expedient way to eliminate an environmental harm in jurisdiction A is to push it over to jurisdiction B.

To return to the shrinking cities phenomenon, if an area's economy is in general decline leading to regional as well as central city population loss, that's one thing, leading to one set of appropriate responses; but, if core city population loss is more indicative of a metro region's hollowing out while the economy remains viable enough to support continued suburban development on the fringe, that's quite another—and one that must be addressed by looking outside the city's jurisdictional borders as well as within. Failure to do so, in my opinion, is simply irresponsible.

# More About Regions

### Multi-jurisdictional Authority and Cooperation in Portland

Metropolitan Portland, Oregon has the nation's only directly elected regional government. First established in 1978, Metro's primary mission is conducting planning and adopting policy to preserve and enhance the quality of life and the environment. This includes authority over transportation investments, land use, and administration of the region's urban growth boundary (outside of which nonrural development generally may not occur), along with regional fish and wildlife habitat protection, and management of some parks and waste management facilities. It has six councilors, each representing a geographic district within the metropolitan area, with one chosen as Metro Council president by his or her peers annually. Metro is served by a staff of 700 employees.

Portland streetcar *(photo courtesy of Reconnecting America)*

Metro's authority is limited to the three Oregon counties in the Portland region, however, and not Clark County, Washington, across the Columbia River. Many credit the stronger authority on the Oregon side with those counties' relatively successful limitation of new development outside the growth boundary: In Clark County, exurban housing grew by 18 percent from 2000 to 2010; by comparison, the Oregon counties added just as many new housing units during the decade but increased the portion outside the growth boundary by only five percent.

The more compact development pattern, supplemented by investment in transportation choices, has brought environmental benefits. Contrary to the national trend, metropolitan Portland's average driving rates (vehicle miles traveled per person per day) have held relatively steady since 1990, while the rate for the nation as a whole increased significantly; Portlanders drive 13 percent fewer miles per day than do average US citizens. Portland has also produced a reduction in carbon emissions from 1990 levels, even though the region has experienced an 18 percent growth in population since then. Residents of Portland emit 35 percent less carbon per capita than those of other US cities.

### California's SB 375

In California, there are no regional governments as such, but a 2008 law (known to most by its bill number, "SB 375") requires the state's metropolitan regions to meet targets for reducing greenhouse gas emissions through land use and transportation measures. In particular, each of the 18 regions' metropolitan planning organizations (all US metro regions have MPOs but few have any regulatory authority) is required to designate growth areas for more efficient housing and commercial development patterns. The areas must be drawn so that they reduce automobile dependence through more walking, more efficient public transit, and shorter driving distances. The land use plan must be supplemented by a complementary transportation network, and the entire "sustainable communities strategy" must be certified as adequate by California's Air Resources Board.

State financial support will flow to transportation projects contained in an approved strategy. Another key element is that individual residential and mixed-use development projects that are consistent with a certified plan will be exempted from certain analytical requirements normally required by the California Environmental Quality Act, since the relevant analysis will already have been performed in the regional planning process. A project found to be a "superior sustainable communities project" under strict environmental and land use criteria will receive additional CEQA exemptions.

Emerging strategies under the law are impressive. The plan for the massive Southern California metro area (the nation's largest by size), for example, calls for investing $246 billion in public transportation; placing 60 percent more housing in transit-accessible locations; placing 87 percent of all jobs within a half mile of transit service; reducing traffic congestion 24 percent per capita despite the addition of four million residents; and saving over 400 square miles of farmland and other open space from development.

## Ontario's Places to Grow Initiative

The North American continent's most impressive plan for managing growth and development, however, may be the *Places to Grow* framework adopted by the province of Ontario, Canada. Constructed pursuant to enabling legislation adopted by the province in 2005, *Places to Grow* addresses the future of a New Hampshire-sized region around and including Toronto, Canada's largest city, and Hamilton, its 8th largest. The plan requires minimum average densities (single-family homes with larger lots may be combined with other housing types to achieve the requisite average) for all new development in the region, with higher densities required for downtowns, transit corridors, and "major transit station areas."

All growth areas must accommodate affordable housing, and development generally may not occur outside of the designated areas. Areas important to natural resources or the environment must be protected, and there are restrictions on development of prime farmland. Perhaps most visibly, the new plan will allow the continued protection of a greenbelt comprising 1.8 million acres of rural and conservation land, an area over three times the size of the Great Smoky Mountains National Park in the US, and just a shade smaller than Yellowstone National Park.

Most impressive of all, *Places to Grow* has the full force and effect of law, thanks to Ontario's Places to Grow Act of 2005. That law requires that local planning decisions, including zoning, conform to the policies in the regional plan. If there is a discrepancy, the provincial government has the authority to amend municipal decisions.

# 2.

# What Seems Green May Actually Be Brown

Near Fredericksburg, Texas *(photo by F. Kaid Benfield)*

Everyone wants to be green these days, especially enterprises that seek to exploit the cachet of sustainability and sell to consumers attracted to a more environmentally friendly lifestyle. The "green" label may be especially appealing if customers don't have to change any of their habits, because the desirable features are embedded in the products or services for sale. But a selective set of facts may conceal the true picture.

The problem is that, in reality, sellers' offerings really can be green in some ways while being "brown," or unsustainable, in others. My favorite example is the phenomenon of so-called "green" buildings located in non-walkable locations that require long car trips for people to get anywhere from them or from anywhere to them.

The truth is that suburban sprawl isn't worthy of the name "green," no matter what environmental bells and whistles are placed on it. In 2010, I reviewed a development called Prairie Ridge Estates, a single-use, single-family residential subdivision being constructed on farmland 40 miles southwest of Chicago. Prairie Ridge's developer billed it as "the nation's first net-zero energy community of custom designed homes," in effect suggesting that, if you purchase a home here, you're as green as it gets. The development's website devoted a page to LEED—the industry-leading green building rating system—featuring the US Green Building Council's LEED logo, and noting the following:

> "In an environment where we face increasing energy costs and have a heightened awareness of environmental responsibility there needs to be an alternative. That alternative is Prairie Ridge Estates, a community of 132 net-zero energy homes in New Lenox, Illinois, that can produce as much energy as a typical family consumes.

> "Built using Insulated Concrete Forms (ICFs), concrete walls encased in a highly engineered insulating foam extend from the foundation to the peaks of the roofline. The homes begin with a shell that is exponentially more efficient than traditional 2"x4" framed houses and are then combined with appliances and technologies that squarely focus on efficiency. From electricity to water to air quality, efficiency has driven the careful and deliberate selection of each window, appliance, and infrastructure system. While a Prairie Ridge Estates home will look and feel just like other homes it will perform unlike any other home, producing its own energy with wind turbines and solar panel systems. The homes also use designed systems, such

as closed-loop geothermal, that limit energy consumption by as much as 80%. The result is a standard LEED Gold certified home that can easily achieve Platinum certification with minor design modifications."

Location of Prairie Ridge Estates *(image from Google Earth)*

So far, so good, I suppose. Those are laudable elements of green building design.

But, um, how can you be "net zero" if you have to drive long distances to do anything? The closest intersection to the Prairie Ridge site that had roads with names in Google's database was the intersection of South Gougar Road (Will County highway 52) and West Oak Avenue (79th Street). That's two-tenths of a mile from the entrance to the subdivision and a third of a mile from the heart. The Walk Score—a measurement of how many shops, services, and amenities are close to any particular address—for that intersection was, well, ZERO when I looked it up. I think that's a different kind of "net zero" than the developer was claiming, though. (The Walk Score remained zero as of early 2013.)

I also ran Prairie Ridge's location through Abogo, a tool developed by the Center for Neighborhood Technology to measure likely transportation costs and transportation-related emissions from any given location: average transportation costs per household were 24 percent higher than the regional average, and carbon emissions from transportation were nearly twice the regional average because of the amount of driving required by the development's sprawl location.

How green does that sound? What might happen to the "net zero" claim if the 1.1 metric tons of carbon dioxide emitted every month by households in the Prairie Ridge location—and the energy consumption they represent—were factored into the equation? And what about the claimed energy cost savings, if you're shelling out $200 more each month for transportation than the average household in your metro region?

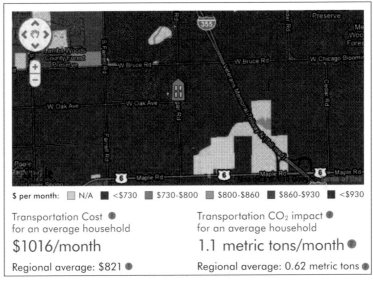

Transportation costs and emissions for Prairie Ridge Estates
*(Abogo image courtesy of Center for Neighborhood Technology)*

According to the website, "lots average 1/3 acre in size. Floorplans start at 2,500 square feet, and lots can accommodate homes as large as 6,000 square feet."

Incidentally, while noodling around Google Earth I found an empty parcel of suburban land about the same size as Prairie Ridge, about four miles away inside the city of Joliet that would have at least brought the Walk Score up to 31, and lower carbon emissions by around 34 percent, compared to Prairie Ridge. A few miles west of the first parcel was another amply-sized suburban tract that would have raised the Walk Score to 66. Both of those were still above the metro regional average in likely transportation costs and emissions, but developing on such "infill" sites in existing communities would at least begin to retrofit suburbia to something more sustainable. If one is aiming for a high level of sustainability, shouldn't such alternative sites be preferred over totally unwalkable sites in the midst of farmland?

Prairie Ridge's environmental shortcomings were not emphasized in the mostly glowing article written about the development in the *Chicago Tribune* in 2010 by Mary Ellen Podmolik. But the writer, to her credit, did observe that "The homeowner's commitment to a green philosophy is a question mark, starting with daily commuting practices: Anyone driving 80 miles round-trip to Chicago in a SUV probably loses the right to claim a green lifestyle." You think? Right across the road from the site is a cornfield.

Location of Prairie Ridge Estates *(image from Google Earth)*

The LEED page on the developer's website mentions, after the passage quoted above, that "LEED for Neighborhood Development extends the benefits of LEED beyond the building footprint into the neighborhood it serves." Well, yes, if you meet the LEED-ND requirements, one of which is that the site be amidst existing development or within walking distance of regular transit service.

In fact, Prairie Ridge is not true green development but exurban sprawl. One can earn LEED building certification pretty much in the middle of nowhere, unfortunately, so this project may well be eligible for a green building certification. Indeed, the developer's first claim was that all of Prairie Ridge's properties would qualify for a gold rating under the LEED for Homes program, and that a builder can make easy adjustments to a building plan to enable a purchaser to aim higher and obtain a platinum rating under the program.

But—speaking as someone who helped write the standards—there is not a chance in hell that Prairie Ridge could earn certification under the more demanding LEED for Neighborhood Development system, which is designed to reward smart, green urbanism. If it does, there is something very wrong with LEED-ND. And I would add that if something in this location, with these transportation characteristics, is awarded a platinum rating under the LEED for Homes criteria, there is something very wrong with that system, too.

## More about "Green"

### The Walmart Conundrum

The giant retail chain Walmart is the world's third largest public corporation, according to the Fortune Global 500 list in 2012. With over two million employees, it is also the biggest private employer in the world and the largest retailer in the world. If you care about the environment, the company is simply too big to ignore.

This point has not been lost on America's mainstream environmental community. Some very good people, including folks I call friends and colleagues, have been working with Walmart to help the company improve its practices. As a result, the retailer has reduced its energy consumption and related greenhouse gas emissions; reduced its consumption of materials and production of waste; and created a "sustainability index" to ensure that the products it sells are increasingly green. The index was described on the company's website this way:

"Our customers desire products that are more efficient, last longer and perform better. They want to know the product's entire lifecycle. They want to know the materials in the product are safe, that it is made well and is produced in a responsible way.

"These desires inspired us to help develop the sustainability index. With this initiative, we are helping create a more transparent supply chain, accelerate the adoption of best practices and drive product innovation and ultimately providing our customers with information they need to assess products' sustainability."

Walmart is requiring its "more than 100,000 global suppliers" to assess their own sustainability in a survey. It is also working with a Sustainability Consortium, funded by the company and administered by two universities, to "develop a global database of information on products' lifecycles—from raw materials to disposal." And it is developing a tool to bring sustainability information to consumers on products sold in Walmarts. The company says its ultimate goal "is to improve the sustainability performance of the products our customers prefer."

Walmart near Burlington, Ontario *(photo courtesy of GFDL)*

These measures deserve our support and applause. To a point.

Green practices, unfortunately, do not make a green company. No matter what environmental progress Walmart is able to make on its materials, supply chains, or resource use, the company maintains an underlying business model that in my opinion has been terrible for the environment and terrible for the sustainability of communities. That business model is predicated on building totally unwalkable facilities on the edge of rural and suburban locations that require driving long distances to take advantage of their "everyday low prices." And it's not just the 200,000-square-foot, low-rise stores; it's also vast suburban parking lots that each contribute upwards of 20 acres of pavement to watersheds; it's the abandonment of these sites after five to ten years when the company moves to newer, bigger locations, farther out of town. And I'm not even getting into labor practices or impacts on local businesses.

The company has earned its "Sprawl-Mart" nickname. To the extent that Walmart has begun to enter more urban markets, as it has here and there, it is doing so in addition to—not instead of—maintaining and expanding its tried and true exurban formula. The sustainability website *care2*, in an article headlined "10 Ways Walmart Fails at Sustainability," criticized the company's land use practices:

> "Despite its public embrace of sustainability, Walmart continues to maximize its land consumption by building vast, low-rise supercenters. Since 2005, Walmart has added more than 1,100 supercenters in the US, expanding its store footprint by one-third. Most of these stores were built on land that hadn't been developed before, including, in some cases, critical habitat for threatened and endangered species.

> "In many communities, Walmart has chosen to build on virgin land rather than redevelop vacant 'grayfield' retail properties [such as older strip malls and sites with obsolete big-box stores]. Walmart itself routinely abandons its stores. The US is currently home to about 150 empty Walmart

stores, many vacated when the chain opened a newer supercenter nearby…

"Yet Walmart's sustainability program does not address land use at all. Its 2012 Global Responsibility Report doesn't even mention these very significant environmental issues."

So, should environmentalists laud the company's very substantial program to reduce its environmental impact? Or should they condemn Walmart for continuing to desecrate the landscape and exacerbate automobile use?

# 3.

# But when Green Elements Align, the Results Can Be Impressive

Grocoff home, Ann Arbor, Michigan *(photo courtesy of Matt Grocoff)*

While green can sometimes be brown—as elaborated in the previous essay—it can also be *really* green, if all the right ingredients are present. This chapter takes a look at a residence that aims high and succeeds.

If the homes in Prairie Ridge Estates (discussed in Chapter 2) are green only when one ignores their sprawling location, Matt and Kelly Grocoff's home in Ann Arbor, Michigan is green in abundance. First, by purchasing an older home (it has now been standing for 112 years), the Grocoffs were able to take advantage of what scientists call "embodied energy," meaning that whatever energy was required to construct the home initially has already been consumed and need not be expended again. In new construction, by contrast, a builder must use energy and release emissions as a result of manufacturing, transportation, and construction of materials. The materials in the Grocoffs' historic home also need not be extracted anew from natural resource lands. Occupancy of the older structure by new residents is the ultimate recycling.

Even more impressively, the family has renovated their home to state-of-the-art energy efficiency standards, including the installation of energy-efficient appliances and household fixtures, the placement of solar panels on the roof, and the use of geothermal heating and cooling. Utility bills demonstrate the results: the household actually generates more energy from on-site renewable sources than it consumes from heating, cooling, lighting, and maintaining the household. The house is not just "net zero" but energy-positive. The Grocoffs believe they have the oldest such home in America.

They aren't stopping there, either. Having conquered the energy issue, the Grocoffs are now taking on water: the next goal is to capture enough rainwater and recycle enough graywater for non-drinking uses to become net zero for water consumption, too.

Moreover, in this case the home is green not only with respect to building energy but also with respect to transportation energy: it is in a walkable city neighborhood amidst other older homes, on compact lots on well-connected streets, with services and amenities close by. All of those characteristics have been proven by research to be associated with reduced driving, reduced carbon emissions, and increased walking and fitness. When I took a look at the house's location on Google Earth, I discovered three schools within a block's walk, and a transit line also a block away. There's a small neighborhood park just down the street. There's a market, a bank branch, and several restaurants within a ten- to twelve-minute walk. Yet the Grocoffs' lot is in a leafy neighborhood of mostly single-family homes.

As I did for Prairie Ridge, I ran the Grocoffs' address through the Center for Neighborhood Technology's Abogo calculator to estimate transportation costs and emissions: I learned that an average household in the Grocoffs' neighborhood emits only half as much carbon from transportation as does an average household for its metropolitan region as a whole. The reduced emissions result not just because of the walkability characteristics mentioned above, but also because the relatively central location shortens driving distances and reduces automobile trips, compared to more outlying subdivisions.

## More About Maximizing Green

### A Look at Some Research

You don't have to take my word for the superior green performance of well-located housing. Among the many studies that have reviewed the effects of neighborhood location on environmental performance is an especially telling one performed by the Jonathan Rose Companies, under a cooperative agreement with the US Environmental Protection Agency. Looking at three different housing types (single-family detached homes, townhomes, and multi-family buildings) and two location types (conventional suburban and transit-oriented urban), the researchers calculated typical energy consumption based on national averages.

They found that the energy consumption (and, thus, greenhouse gas emissions) of a typical household in a transit-oriented location is likely to be less than that of a similarly sized household in a conventional suburban location, *even if the household in the conventional suburban location is assisted by energy-efficient building technology and fuel-efficient vehicles*. The most energy efficiency and greenhouse gas reduction occurs, of course, if the household is given both a transit-oriented location *and* the benefit of green building and vehicle technology.

Consider the somewhat complicated series of bar graphs on the next page. Combining the BTUs (British Thermal Units, a measure of energy use that correlates with greenhouse gas emissions) required for both transportation and building energy for

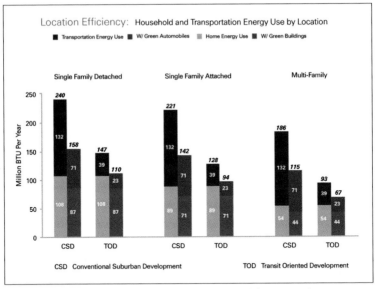

Location Efficiency: Household and Transportation Energy Use by Location

■ Transportation Energy Use  ■ W/ Green Automobiles  ■ Home Energy Use  ■ W/ Green Buildings

Approximate energy consumed under various household scenarios *(Image courtesy of Jonathan Rose Companies and US Environmental Protection Agency)*

each household type and location, the graph indicates the effects of different combinations. On the far left, for example, the most energy-intensive household type is the single-family, detached house in a conventional suburban location; most of its energy use (132 million BTU per year, on average) is for transportation; the rest (108 million BTU per year) is for building and appliances operation. Counting both forms of energy use, the home requires an average of 240 million BTU per year.

The graph shows that, if we give that same household the benefits of energy-efficient building technology and fuel-efficient vehicles, we can reduce its energy footprint from 240 to 158 million BTU per year. That reduction is not insignificant. But simply putting the very same household in a more central, transit-served location, without any building or vehicle greening whatever, would reduce BTU requirements even further, to 147 million BTU per year. The location improvement outperforms the technology improvement. To do even better still, give the single-family household in the transit-oriented location green building features and green vehicles, and we're down to 110 million BTU per year, only 46 percent of the energy required for the conventional single family detached home in the conventional suburban location.

The same sort of comparison yields similar results for single-family attached homes (townhouses, the middle pair of bars on the graph) and for multi-family homes (condos or apartments, the far right bars on the graph). On the far right, the graph shows that a multi-family home in a transit-oriented location with green building features and energy-efficient vehicles generates the lowest energy usage of all, 67 million BTU per year, only 28 percent of that required by the conventionally located and designed single-family home.

| | Energy-efficient home and car | Transit-oriented location | Energy-efficient home and car in a transit-friendly site |
|---|---|---|---|
| A household in this type of home in a conventional suburban location can reduce its energy consumption by... | | | |
| Single-family detached home | 34 percent | 39 percent | 54 percent |
| Single-family attached home (rowhouse or townhouse) | 35 percent | 42 percent | 57 percent |
| Multi-family home | 38 percent | 50 percent | 54 percent |
| | ...just by adopting energy efficiency measurements in its home and driving a fuel-efficient car. | ...just by being located in a transit-friendly site. | ...by making its home and car more energy efficient and being on a site that is close to transit. |

Approximate energy savings from changes in household circumstances
*(image courtesy of US Environmental Protection Agency)*

To explain further, EPA has created a flowchart that indicates the various increments of energy efficiency improvement one can achieve by moving along the spectrum from totally conventional households to the most highly efficient households when both transportation and building energy are considered. The analysis isn't perfect, of course, since real world situations vary and may not be captured fully in a comparison based on averages. (The Grocoff household would beat the green performance of any of these scenarios by a considerable margin.) There are also assumptions, based on research and judgment, that go into the analysis. The peer reviewers did not find any of them to be unreasonable. The analysis was published in 2011.

The upshot? We cannot fully address energy use and carbon emissions problems by looking only at building and vehicle technology; we also have to look at land use and transit availability.

# 4.

# Revitalization Can
# Be Powerful

Revitalization of Crown Square, St. Louis *(photo courtesy of Old North Restoration Group)*

When revitalization of our distressed neighborhoods is done
well, it is almost unrivaled in its ability to advance simultaneously
the "triple bottom line" goals of sustainability: improving the
environment, the economy, and social equity. To understand
why, we must first consider why cities, once seen as a source of
environmental problems, can be better understood as a source
of environmental solutions. Making cities stronger and greener
is a key to a sustainable future.

America's environmental community was initially built on the celebration of wilderness and the rural landscape as a more romantic and pastoral antidote to cities and towns. Thoreau's Walden Pond and John Muir's Yosemite Valley were seen as the ideal, while cities were seen as sources of dirt and pollution, something to get away from. If environmentalists were involved with cities at all, it was likely to be in efforts to oppose new development, with the effect of making our built environment more spread out, and less urban.

We've come a long way since then, if still not far enough. We were and remain right to uphold nature, wildlife, and the rural landscape as places critical to celebrate, preserve, and withdraw to. But what we realize now, many of us anyway, is that cities and towns— the communities where for millennia people have congregated in search of more efficient commerce, resource sharing, and social networks—hold our greatest hope for sustaining the rural landscape. The best way to save wilderness is through compact, beautiful communities that are more, not less, urban and do not encroach on places of significant natural value.

For our cities and towns to function as successful people habitat, though, they must be communities where people *want* to live, work, and play. We must make them great, but always within a decidedly urban, nonsprawling form. (This does not always mean high-rises, as discussed in Chapter 11.) As it turns out, compact living—in communities of streets, homes, shops, workplaces, schools, and the like assembled at a walkable scale—not only helps to save the landscape, it also reduces pollution and consumption of resources. We don't drive as far or as often; we share infrastructure.

Recent authors such as Edward Glaeser (*The Triumph of the City*) and David Owen (*Green Metropolis*) are sometimes excessive in extolling the virtues of urban density without giving attention to the other things that make cities attractive and successful. But they are absolutely right that city living reduces per-person energy consumption, carbon emissions, and other negative environmental effects.

A lot of my professional friends are committed urbanists as well as committed environmentalists. We appreciate the environmental advantages of urban living so thoroughly that we can take it for granted that other people feel the same. But we make that mistake at our—and the planet's—peril. Sustainable cities and towns will not become the norm without a concerted effort that takes others' needs and preferences into account and meets them in more sustainable ways.

A lot is riding on the outcome: Despite the sluggish economy in recent years, America's population is projected to increase by 70 million people and 50 million households over the next 25 to 30 years, the equivalent of adding France or Germany to the US. Between building new homes, workplaces, shops, and schools and replacing those that will have reached the end of their functional lives, fully half the built environment that will be on the ground in three decades does not yet exist.

Housing development near Tucson, Arizona *(photo courtesy of Daniel Lobo)*

We cannot continue to spread out as we have in the recent past. Our sprawling pattern of development has done a lot of damage, particularly in the latter half of the 20th century, when America severely disinvested our inner cities and traditional towns while population, investment, and tax base fled for (quite literally) greener pastures. The result, as we now know all too well, has been desecration of the natural and rural landscape, decaying city infrastructure, polluted air and waterways, and distressed populations.

Older cities and towns with shrinking revenues did what they could to maintain services, but critical issues such as waste, public transportation, street and sidewalk maintenance, parks, libraries, and neighborhood schools—issues where attention and investment could have made a difference—were often back-burnered or neglected altogether. Meanwhile, sprawl caused driving rates to grow three times faster than population, sending carbon and other emissions through the roof while requiring costly new infrastructure to be built while we neglected the old.

Today, we need our inner cities and older communities to absorb as much of our anticipated growth as possible, to keep the impacts per increment of expected growth as low as we can. And, to do that, we must bring cities back to life, with great neighborhoods and complete streets, with walkability and well-functioning public transit, with clean parks and rivers, with air that is safe to breathe and water that is safe to drink. This is the essence of revitalization.

Where cities have been disinvested, we must rebuild them; where populations have been neglected, we must provide them with opportunity; where suburbs have been allowed to sprawl nonsensically, we must retrofit them and make them better. These are not just economic and social matters: these are environmental issues, every bit as deserving of the environmental community's attention as the preservation of nature.

Revitalization poses risks for social equity, unfortunately. Without proper attention to the issue residents may not be able to afford to stay in a neighborhood that becomes more expensive, breaking important bonds between people and between people and place. But, when done thoughtfully, revitalization can benefit distressed populations. Sections of the South Bronx in New York City, for example, had become severely abandoned and literally burnt-out by the late 1980s. But a group of remaining citizens, all low-income, formed a group called Nos Quedamos ("we are staying") and worked with the city to plan the recovery of their own neighborhood, which is now thriving. In Missouri, the Old North Saint Louis Restoration Group joined a highly diverse group of longtime and newer residents to jointly plan the rebirth of a large section of the city that had declined from 40,000 residents to around 2,000. Other inclusive and highly successful regeneration efforts can be found in Boston, Denver, Los Angeles, Oakland, Chicago, and other cities.

While many developers and municipalities fail to take advantage, I think helping disinvested neighborhoods recover and prosper from the inside is where the real excitement is when it comes to making more sustainable places.

## More about Revitalization

### Using LEED for Neighborhood Development to Improve Recovering Neighborhoods

Revitalization happens at the neighborhood scale. As discussed in Chapter 1, neighborhoods are where increments of development take place and where most people connect with their cities, their environments, and each other on an everyday basis.

Between 2002 and 2009, three nonprofit organizations—the Natural Resources Defense Council, the Congress for the New Urbanism, and the United States Green Building Council—made a major investment to help improve the shape and character of American development at the neighborhood scale. The result was LEED for Neighborhood Development (LEED is the US Green Building Council's acronym for Leadership in Energy and Environmental Design), the first set of consensus-based national standards to guide new development to the right places with the right sustainable design. The goal of the program was, and continues to be, to define what is smart about so-called "smart growth" and what is green about green neighborhoods, so that the private sector, public officials, and citizens alike will be able to evaluate and encourage the right kind of development. (The US Green Building Council now administers the program.)

A revitalizing neighborhood in Boston aims for LEED-ND gold
*(photo by F. Kaid Benfield)*

The aspiration of LEED-ND certification was to provide a boost for good development proposals while they were being considered, along with a set of model standards that could be adapted by governments and others who were also seeking to encourage sustainability. The aspiration has indeed been met: notwithstanding continuing turmoil in the real estate and development industry, over 100 exemplary projects have now been certified under the LEED-ND pilot and the more recent version of the program, from Vancouver's urban Olympic Village (now a mixed-use community), to green affordable housing in Savannah, to a revitalizing arts district in Syracuse.

In addition, while LEED-ND was intended primarily to influence the private sector, the program has earned increasing government recognition, with incorporation into public policy instruments ranging from a state incentive program in Illinois to new city plans in El Paso, Texas, and Bellingham, Washington, to the discretionary grant programs of the US Department of Housing and Urban Development, which is now using LEED-ND criteria in its evaluation process.

The LEED-ND program was designed from the very beginning to be especially supportive of revitalization and infill development in our inner cities and older communities. In 2011, the Natural Resources Defense Council joined with the Local Initiatives Support Corporation and other partners in an effort to help selected inner-city neighborhoods around the country plan a more sustainable future. More specifically, the partnership is using the structure and standards of LEED-ND to help community development corporations in low-income urban districts do the following:

- Locate, design, and build new investments to a sustainability standard sufficient to achieve LEED-ND certification at a high level (including walkable, mixed-use features; transportation choices; access to parks, healthy food, jobs, and schools; and advanced techniques for energy and water management);
- Involve local residents to the greatest extent possible in planning and design, and ensure that there is no net loss in affordable housing;
- Apply environmental analysis to quantify the benefits we hope to achieve; and
- Develop replicable approaches that can be transferred to additional CDCs and municipalities around the country.

As I write, the partnership has already begun providing technical and financial assistance to efforts in Philadelphia, Indianapolis, Boston, Los Angeles, and Ithaca, NY.

# 5.

# In a Revitalizing District, Some Gentrification Might Be OK; but Not Too Much

Café in revitalizing St. Louis neighborhood *(photo courtesy of Old North Restoration Group)*

So-called "white flight" to the suburbs during the latter part of the 20th century was catastrophic for inner cities, leaving mostly minority populations behind to suffer from a prolonged lack of investment, opportunity, and a tax base sufficient to support decent public services. It is understandable that, having been burned more than once by affluent populations, current city dwellers of modest means are suspicious of well-to-do newcomers who have recently discovered the advantages of urban life.

I undertake this topic with more than a little trepidation, since it is by its nature emotionally and, not infrequently, racially charged. The title is deliberately chosen but somewhat rhetorical, since whether one agrees with the proposition ultimately depends on one's definition of "gentrification." But the truth is that many neighborhoods are destined to remain underserved pockets of concentrated poverty unless new taxpayers are accepted.

As discussed in Chapter 4, most urban thinkers agree that the massive abandonment and resulting disinvestment of large areas of our cities by the (largely white) middle class, beginning in the 1960s and only recently reversing in many places, was terrible for cities, for populations left behind, and for the environment. But many residents whose families remained through those years of disinvestment and until the present day are understandably fearful that addressing these problems by bringing new residents and economic activity into their neighborhoods will only benefit the newcomers while disadvantaging the existing community. The biggest fear is that current residents will be displaced to make room for redevelopment.

There is a political dimension, too, as African-American and other nonwhite populations gained a majority of the voting power in many districts and cities after whites left. Indeed, in 1950, the city of Washington, DC was 65 percent white; by 1970, it was 71 percent black, an astounding change. "Chocolate City" became an expression of ethnic pride.

But, as whites return, the ability of minorities to influence civic affairs and protect important interests may be diminished. (Sometimes lost in the equation is that African-Americans are losing population and influence in central cities not only to white return but also to middle-class "black flight" in recent years to suburbs perceived to be safer and to have better schools.) The result of more recent changes is that, in 2010, African Americans composed only 50.7 percent of the city's population, the rest mostly white (38.5 percent) or Hispanic (9.1 percent). (The racial composition of the metropolitan area as a whole in 2010 was 55 percent white, 26 percent black, 14 percent Hispanic, 9 percent Asian, and 4 percent "mixed and other.")

While longtime residents may seldom express it this way, I think a big part of their concern about the city becoming whiter and more affluent stems not just from worries about affordability and displacement but also from the perception that the changes are not coming from within their community. They feel that they are losing control over their neighborhoods.

Elections now can be won or lost on these issues, as former Washington, DC mayor Adrian Fenty could possibly attest. Fenty's administration pushed school reform, bike lanes, revitalization and streetcars, all of which were to one degree or another associated with a gentrification agenda by many city residents. Even dog parks became a symbolic issue associated with newcomers in revitalizing neighborhoods. Fenty (whose father is African-American) was tossed out, with voters split along racial lines.

DC's Capital Bikeshare program *(photo courtesy of DC Department of Transportation)*

After the primary, *Washington Post* columnist Courtland Milloy could hardly contain his gleeful contempt for the loser. He leveled many charges at Fenty in his celebratory column, not all of them unfair in my opinion. I'm not so sure about this one, though, laced with sarcasm:

"As for you blacks: Don't you, like, even know what's good for you? So what if Fenty reneged on his promise to strengthen the city from the inside by helping the working poor move into the middle class? Nobody cares that he has opted to import a middle class, mostly young whites who can afford to pay high rent for condos that replaced affordable apartments.

"Don't ask Fenty or [former DC school chancellor Michelle] Rhee whom this world-class school system will serve if low-income black residents are being evicted from his world-class city in droves."

While many would dispute the hyperbole, Milloy was nonetheless expressing the sentiments of a substantial part of the city's electorate. The return of middle-class whites to once-disinvested neighborhoods presents a tough, tough set of circumstances in which it can be hard to remain rational.

My own belief is that we should be working for revitalization that encourages mixed-income neighborhoods in which new residents and businesses are welcomed while displacement is avoided or minimized. But make no mistake: that revitalization must continue to take place in America's cities. It is absolutely essential if we are to have any hope of a more sustainable tax base to fund civic restoration and improvement, a more equitable civil society, and a more environmentally sustainable pattern of growth that reduces sprawling consumption of the landscape while bringing down our rates of driving emissions (central locations with moderate or greater density and nearby conveniences facilitate walking, transit, and shorter driving distances).

Fortunately, there are some great neighborhoods that seem to be revitalizing in the right way. I mentioned a few in the previous chapter, and I could add others across the country from Oakland and Seattle to Denver, from Chicago and Indianapolis to New Haven. Residents of some great city communities are demonstrating that they can be fully committed to their community's revitalization and to shaping it rather than opposing it. All are achieving levels of success, though the national real estate slump of the last several years hasn't helped any.

The truth is that what some badly disinvested cities, districts, and neighborhoods desperately need is some amount of "gentrification." The challenge is to have enough without having too much, to have new development that continues to meet the needs of existing populations as well as newcomers.

To that point, Jeremy Borden wrote in a 2011 article in *The Washington Post* about residents who had formed a community development task force to influence the shape of revitalization along the city's Georgia Avenue corridor, a major north-south thoroughfare. Lined mostly with mid-rise buildings and small, storefront businesses, Georgia Avenue was once the scene of mass riots and crime but now is poised for an update. A historic theater is being restored and a new, mixed-use development will house, among other tenants, The United Negro College Fund. Kent Boese reported on the *Greater Greater Washington* blog that, for its part, the city was contributing an $8 million "Great Streets" infrastructure upgrade, which will improve and replace sidewalks, install new trash cans and park benches, install "historically sympathetic" street lighting and signals, create textured crosswalks, improve two parks, and install green infrastructure to manage stormwater.

As I write, several additional important projects are also on the table, including major redevelopment on the site of the famous but recently closed Walter Reed Army Medical Center; a campus plan for Howard University, along with the nearby Howard Town Center development; and a controversial Walmart.

The Georgia Avenue Walmart, one of six potentially to be built in DC, could unfortunately pose a threat to just the kinds of businesses that the city and residents are hoping to attract and support. An economic impact analysis prepared by Public and Environmental Finance Associates and filed with the city found that "there is every reason to anticipate" that the store "will cause substantial diversion of sales from existing businesses in…immediate and nearby neighborhoods, and from elsewhere in the District," particularly increas-

ing the probability that existing supermarkets could close as a result
of lost business. Nonetheless, the city's planning office found the
Walmart proposal "not inconsistent" with the city's comprehensive
plan, and is allowing the massive store to go forward, apparently con-
cluding that impact on current businesses is not an issue the office is
allowed to consider in the review process.

New construction in Washington, DC *(photo courtesy of Daniel Lobo)*

More hopeful for Georgia Avenue and existing corridor residents, perhaps, is a report that the city is considering building the
corridor's new streetcar line, which had been back-burnered, sooner
rather than later. In the meantime, the community development
task force has created a history trail and is sprucing up blank walls
with murals and empty storefronts with art projects. The idea is
to bring a sense of pride and progress that will make the neighborhood more pleasant while helping to attract the right kind of
investment. "We do want new people along Georgia Avenue," one
of the task force leaders told Borden, "But we want to make sure
that the people who want to stay can stay and shape Georgia Avenue in the way we want." Bingo. I'm hoping that the task force will

be a strong, responsible, and influential voice as new businesses and people come to the corridor.

Even at its best, though, revitalization can be messy, as well as dependent on the local legal framework and economic context. And the reality is that the "middle class, mostly young whites" disparaged in Courtland Milloy's election gloating are going to be critical to any urban resurgence. In his always-thoughtful blog *Rebuilding Place in the Urban Space*, Richard Layman describes some of the reasons:

> "[F]or the past 20 years…DC's black population has been dropping—in large part as the black middle classes decamped to the suburbs, abandoning the city, just as the whites had done in the 1950s.

> "If not for an influx of white and Hispanic residents, DC's population would have steadily declined over the past 20 years because of black outmigration."

While I haven't researched the numbers to discern the extent to which Washington's changing demographics reflect those of other cities, I think they suggest a likely universal truth: We need cities that are capable of attracting diverse new residents with incomes that can strengthen the tax base and support new economic activity, but that are also strong and hospitable enough to hold on to existing residents. And we must provide both groups of residents with the services and amenities required to meet their needs. Is that too much to hope for? I think that getting there is going to be a rough and rocky road, but I am optimistic for the long run.

Fashioning the more equitable, prosperous, and sustainable cities of the future will require more, not less, revitalization and more, not fewer, new residents. But it will also require providing high-quality affordable housing in neighborhoods where revitalization is occurring. It will require bringing existing residents to the table early and often in the planning process, but to help shape good neighborhood development, not to prevent it. And, where wounds over gentrification exist, we must take steps to heal them, because divisive rhetoric only hurts everyone involved and, ultimately, the viability of our communities.

# More about Changing City Demographics

### Do Current Trends Support Families?

In DC, as it turns out, recent growth in the inner city has been a certain kind of growth. Jonathan O'Connell, in a lengthy and especially insightful 2012 article in *The Washington Post*, observed that the demographic most associated with the city's remarkable turn-around comprises ambitious young professionals without kids. Indeed, a census analysis published in 2011 showed that almost all of the city's population increase since 2000 can be accounted for by an increase in residents between 20 and 35 years old. The number of children younger than 15 dropped by a fifth.

O'Connell wondered whether the city can hold onto its new residents as they mature:

> "During the past decade, Washington has become a magnet for ambitious 20-somethings. Not only does the city offer good jobs and better-than-average public transit, it also boasts food trucks and, of course, cupcake shops… The influx of newcomers has transformed the city from a symbol of civic dysfunction and drab government offices to a cosmopolitan hub—an urban playground.

> "The flood of newcomers did not arrive by accident. City planners and developers have bet big on luring transplants to the region. These are the people who will fill the more than 11,000 new apartments expected to be completed in the area in the next 12 months and whose income, sales and real estate taxes are helping the city's finances fare far better than those of similar urban areas. Long-blighted storefronts and commercial corridors are being rebuilt.

"What D.C. hasn't yet figured out, or even really planned for, is what happens when this raft of newcomers grows out of one-bedroom condo living. What happens when their lives evolve past the urban-playground stage and they are less interested in speakeasies than in parks for their kids?"

Excellent question. And there are also the matters of public education and safety. My sense is that the city's schools are, in fact, getting better, but slowly, and maybe not fast enough for residents starting families and having choices about where to live. As for crime, DC is much, much safer than it was, say, 20 years ago; but the parts of the city that are most rapidly urbanizing include some neighborhoods that are still sketchy for kids.

O'Connell offers three pragmatic recommendations that he believes can help the city do a better job of accommodating young families:

- Develop places—public and private—where children can eat and play, something many District neighborhoods lack. Family-friendly restaurants are critical, but right now DC is building bars more quickly.
- Diversify the housing stock. Incentives for developers to build larger units would provide more housing options for families.
- Build parks along with new residential development.

Those seem almost ridiculously sensible to me, if also a bit modest. Implementing them would be a start, at least.

# 6.

# Cities Need Nature

Russell Square, London *(photo by F. Kaid Benfield)*

We humans have an intrinsic emotional need to connect with nature. The eminent biologist E. O. Wilson first called our affinity for the natural world "biophilia," and the term has stuck. Yet cities also, and fundamentally, need the structure of hardscape urbanism—streets, buildings, and infrastructure—in sufficient density to achieve environmental and economic efficiency and nurture social bonds. It is critical that we incorporate nature into cities, but we must do so in a way that supports urbanity rather than replaces it.

I remember a happy day in our neighborhood a few years back. When I came home from work, three new trees had been planted on our block. That's a small thing, of course, just three street trees. But their predecessors had been sorely missed for a few years. When we moved into the neighborhood a little over 20 years ago, one of its major assets was large, stately street trees, most of them oaks, on nearly every block. The neighborhood was built in the 1920s, so our oldest trees would have been around 70 years old when we moved in.

Visitors are always struck by them, especially if they have come from a newer suburb. Many of those older trees remain, but over the time that we have lived in the neighborhood we have lost quite a few to disease and, mostly, storms. I'm sure I was not the only one whose spirits were lifted by the discovery that new ones had been planted: researchers have shown that even just a view of greenery from a window can give us a psychological and physical boost.

Indeed, for our ancestors a keen awareness of the natural environment was essential to survival. When we are deprived of nature, we lose a basic aspect of humanity. Who among us has not enjoyed a stroll, ridden a bike, read a book or magazine, learned a sport, fallen in love, taken a nap, or otherwise enjoyed the respite and communion with nature provided by a natural area or lovely city park? In cities, the presence of nature—whether interspersed among our streets, buildings, and yards or more organized into parks—connects us with growth and with the seasons, providing a softness to complement the concrete of our streets and sidewalks and the brick and wood of our houses.

Among parks, I love those that are neighborhood-scaled the most. While large green spaces such as New York's Central Park, San Francisco's Golden Gate Park, or Washington, DC's Rock Creek Park are wonderful, there is a more personal dimension to those that are a bit smaller, more a part of their neighborhoods. Indeed, one of my favorites is only about an acre and a half in size. It's tucked into a neighborhood of single-family homes on small lots in Chevy Chase, Maryland, right on the boundary separating Chevy Chase from Bethesda and only a block from Bethesda's very busy and urban main street.

Elm Street Park is so well scaled to its neighborhood and has such beautiful large, mature trees that I go out of my way to stop there if I'm riding my bike nearby, which I do often. There are small gazebos, a playground, and scattered picnic tables but otherwise it has no special facilities. It's just there, and I love it.

## The Science of Urban Nature and People Habitat

Research suggests that I should. At the University of Michigan, a test group of students walking through an urban arboretum scored better on memory and mood indicia than a control group walking on city streets. When the roles of the two groups were reversed a week later, the students who walked through the arboretum again scored higher. The researchers suggested that the additional mental demands of with city streets—particularly attention to cars—caused stress, while in nature we can let our minds wander, enabling us to "rest our attention."

More broadly, an academically rigorous review of 86 peer-reviewed studies published since 2000, conducted by Danish researchers for the International Federation of Parks and Recreation Administration, was published in January 2013. It found an immense range of correlations between nature and public health, from reduced headaches to longevity:

> "Nature and green spaces contribute directly to public health by reducing stress and mental disorders, increasing the effect of physical activity, reducing health inequalities, and increasing perception of life quality and self-reported general health. Indirect health effects are conveyed by providing arenas and opportunities for physical activity, increasing satisfaction of living environment and social interactions, and by different modes of recreation…

> "The direct health benefits for which we found evidence on positive effects included psychological well-being, reduced obesity, reduced stress, self-perceived health,

reduced headache, better mental health, stroke mortality,
concentration capacity, quality of life, reduced Attention
Disorder Hyperactivity Disorder (ADHD) symptoms,
reduced cardiovascular symptoms and reduced mortality
for respiratory disorders, reduced health complaints, overall
mortality, longevity, birth weight and gestational age in
low socioeconomic population, post-disaster recovery, and
reduced cortisol." [Citations omitted.]

The evidence for positive impacts of urban parks on physical activity was highlighted as "strong," with the academically established
evidence in support of other effects found to be at least "moderate."
(Conversely, when a correlation between parks and health was in-
sufficiently established in the literature, as with the effects on lung
cancer or diabetes, the authors said so.)

Elm Street Park, Chevy Chase, Maryland *(photo by F. Kaid Benfield)*

Another large study, reported in a monograph published by the
National Recreation and Park Association in 2010, found a direct
correlation between health effects and proximity of parks:

"Scientists in the Netherlands examined the prevalence of
anxiety disorders in more than 345,000 residents and found

that people who lived in residential areas with the least green spaces had a 44 percent higher rate of physician-diagnosed anxiety disorders than people who lived in the greenest residential areas. The effect was strongest among those most likely to spend their time near home, including children and those with low levels of education and income.

"Time spent in the lushness of green environments also reduces sadness and depression. In the Dutch study, the prevalence of physician-diagnosed depression was 33 percent higher in the residential areas with the fewest green spaces, compared to the neighborhoods with the most."

The NRPA report even cites studies finding lower levels of aggression, violence, and crime in Chicago housing projects with views of vegetation than in those without.

People intuitively appreciate these benefits and, as a result, are willing to pay a significant premium for living near nature. According to a 2006 report published by the Trust for Public Land, a review of 25 studies investigating whether parks and open space contributed to values of neighboring properties found increased value in 20 of the studies. Those benefits accrue to the municipalities as well:

"The higher value of these homes means that their owners pay higher property taxes. In some instances, the additional property taxes are sufficient to pay the annual debt charges on the bonds used to finance the park's acquisition and development. 'In these cases, the park is obtained at no long-term cost to the jurisdiction,' [Texas A&M professor John] Crompton writes."

The TPL report cites corroborating evidence from the University of Southern California, finding that investment in a pocket park in a dense urban neighborhood would pay for itself in 15 years as a result of increased tax revenues.

# Environmental Services Provided by Urban Nature

Back to the trees in my neighborhood, I would love them without knowing why but, in my day job as an advocate, it's very useful to know that science can reveal some of the reasons. Apart from what they may do for me, trees also provide measurable environmental services to their communities. If you're interested in learning more about the benefits of trees, visit the websites of the National Arbor Day Foundation and the US Forest Service. Among the tidbits I have discovered on one or the other of those two sites are these:

- The net cooling effect of a young, healthy tree is equivalent to ten room-size air conditioners operating 20 hours a day.
- If you plant a tree today on the west side of your home, in 5 years your energy bills should be 3 percent less. In 15 years the savings will be nearly 12 percent.
- One acre of forest absorbs six tons of carbon dioxide and puts out four tons of oxygen.
- A number of studies have shown that real estate agents and home buyers assign between 10 and 23 percent of the value of a residence to the trees on the property.
- Surgery patients who could see a grove of deciduous trees recuperated faster and required less pain-killing medicine than similar patients who viewed only brick walls.
- In one study, stands of trees reduced particulates by 9 to 13 percent, and reduced the amount reaching the ground below by 27 to 42 percent compared to an open area.

Several years ago walkability guru Dan Burden, who founded the Pedestrian and Bicycle Information Center, wrote a detailed monograph titled *22 Benefits of Urban Street Trees*. Among other things, Burden calculated that "for a planting cost of $250-600 (includes first 3 years of maintenance) a single street tree returns over $90,000 of direct benefits (not including aesthetic, social and natural) in the lifetime of the tree." He cites data finding that street trees create slower and more appropriate urban traffic speeds, increase customer attraction to businesses, and obviate increments of costly drainage infrastructure. In at least two recent studies (reported after Burden's analysis), trees were even found to be associated with reduced crime.

4-way duty as tree cover, street median, stormwater catchment, and pocket park
*(photo by F. Kaid Benfield)*

Burden summarizes trees' biological and emotional functions:

"Urban street trees provide a canopy, root structure and setting for important insect and bacterial life below the surface; at grade for pets and romantic people to pause for what pets and romantic people pause for; they act as essential lofty environments for song birds, seeds, nuts, squirrels and other urban life. Indeed, street trees so well establish natural and comfortable urban life it is unlikely we will ever see any advertisement for any marketed urban product, including cars, to be featured without street trees making the ultimate dominant, bold visual statement about place."

Intuitively if not explicitly, street trees remind us that, even in the city, we are a part of living nature. They connect us to something larger and wondrous, yet protective and comforting. They remind us that we are creatures in a habitat, and that is a very good thing.

## The Emerging Field of Green Infrastructure

Urban greenery can also help control water pollution. An increasingly popular set of techniques is called "green infrastructure," in the form of strategically designed vegetation and landscaping to filter stormwater (while also lowering summer temperatures and releasing oxygen).

The stormwater control provided by green infrastructure is significant. One of the most pressing environmental challenges facing cities and suburbs in the US is the impact of rainfall that becomes polluted runoff when it flows over impervious surfaces—such as highways, parking lots, rooftops and driveways—on its way into our rivers, lakes, and coastal waters. The federal EPA estimates that more than 10 trillion gallons of untreated urban and suburban stormwater runoff enters our surface waters each year, degrading recreation, destroying fish habitat, and altering stream ecology and hydrology.

Capitol Avenue, Hartford, before *(courtesy of US Environmental Protection Agency)*

The problem becomes particularly acute in cities that drain both stormwater and sewage into a common, and typically aging, set of pipes and conveyances. When major storm events prove to be more than these systems can handle, the result is "combined sewer overflows," a noxious mess.

Green infrastructure (also known as the key component of "low impact development") captures and filters stormwater before it runs off into sewers or urban waterways. It replicates the way nature deals with precipitation—using vegetation and soils as natural sponges for runoff—rather than relying exclusively on the "gray infrastructure" of old technology, such as concrete pipes and holding tanks. Types of green infrastructure include green roofs, roadside plantings, rain gardens, permeable paving, and rainwater harvesting, among others.

The American Society of Landscape Architects maintains a massive database containing hundreds of case studies of successful examples, half of which are placed within existing development. Another sizable batch involves urban redevelopment projects. The organization has found that the use of green infrastructure reduces development costs more frequently than it adds them, probably

Capitol Avenue, Hartford, as imagined *(courtesy of US Environmental Protection Agency)*

because successful green infrastructure can obviate some of the concrete "gray infrastructure" otherwise required to drain runoff.

Bioswales were the most common type employed, with rain gardens and porous pavers close behind. Of all of the profiled projects, 40 percent reflected the management of an acre or less of land; 75 percent were employed on five acres or less. Sixty-eight percent of the projects were assisted with public funds.

Philadelphia is perhaps the country's leading example of a city committed to large-scale green infrastructure implementation. Under a formal plan to meet Clean Water Act requirements, approved by environmental regulators, the city has now agreed to transform at least one-third of the impervious areas served by its sewer system into "greened acres"—spaces that use green infrastructure to infiltrate, or otherwise collect, the first inch of runoff from any storm. My colleagues at the Natural Resources Defense Council say the program will keep 80-90% of annual rainfall from these areas out of Philadelphia's over-burdened sewer system.

In a different undertaking, the federal Environmental Protection Agency has launched an innovative planning program designed to help bring more green infrastructure (and green building practices) to our country's state capitals, making them simultaneously more environmentally resilient and more beautiful. The idea behind *Greening America's Capitals* is that these particularly prominent cities are inevitably ambassadors of a sort for their respective states and for other cities.

Indeed, elected representatives and their staffs typically come from all around their respective states but work at least part-time every year in the capital cities. What they experience there, good or bad, imparts lessons that can be taken back to the representatives' home districts or even incorporated into statewide policy. Many visitors frequent state capitals for business or pleasure, each forming and taking away impressions. I took a close look at the EPA-assisted plan for greening Hartford, Connecticut and was seriously impressed.

As I have written often, smart growth—growing our metropolitan regions in more compact patterns—does its own part in reducing the volume of runoff across watersheds, because it reduces the spread of new pavement into previously undeveloped or minimally developed areas. But it is not enough, because we need waterways near our existing developed areas to become cleaner and safer. Many cities and suburbs are now undergoing more intensive development, as they must to address other environmental concerns such as transportation efficiency and land conservation. We clearly need urban density in order to even approach solving problems related to land conservation and transportation patterns and emissions. But, if the development is not sensitive to the potential for runoff, some waterways could become even more polluted.

I have become a big fan of green infrastructure because these techniques—in most cases literally as well as figuratively green—have the effect of softening urban density, making it more appealing as well as better functioning. In fact, I would argue that, in places where there is significant rainfall, smart growth simply isn't smart without it.

## More about City Greenery

### Perhaps My Favorite City Park

Whenever I am lucky enough to be in Paris, I always make a point to stay within easy walking distance of that city's wonderful *Jardin du Luxembourg* (Luxembourg Garden). When my wife and I are there together, we spend a little time there almost every day. It's one of my favorite public spaces in the world.

What makes it work so well? I can think of a few things right away: First, it's a great size for a large city park, at 60 acres. That means one still feels "in the city" when there, but in an especially tranquil part. Second, like great cities themselves, it embodies a variety of vistas and experiences, from the majestic old Luxembourg Palace (now the seat of the French Senate), to the central pond where kids play with toy boats, to a bandstand, a marionette theater, a carrousel, tennis courts, the Medici fountain, terrific nooks and crannies in which to eat and drink, and so on.

Third, it strikes a great balance by nearly always hosting a good crowd while avoiding the feeling that it is jammed with people, in the sense that, say, Bryant Park or parts of Central Park in New York City do. There's almost always a place to sit. Fourth, the buildings and landscape architecture are humane rather than heroic or pastoral, and to my eyes, beautiful. In addition, as with many great places in Europe, the park conveys a sense of history (it's been there since 1625) that few places close to home can match.

Jardin du Luxembourg, Paris *(photo by F. Kaid Benfield)*

But don't take my word for it. Here's what the Project for Public Spaces has to say:

> "The Luxembourg Garden may well be one of the most
> successful parks in the world, partly because it is so well
> integrated into the fabric of the city around it, which makes
> it easily accessible. There are also many things to do there,
> evidenced by the wide range of people who use it: children,
> older people, Sorbonne students, people cutting through
> on a lunch break, etc. People come to stroll, play chess, to
> sit and read, people watch, to sit at one of the cafes or to
> bring their children or grandchildren to one of the many
> attractions for kids. Organized activities at the park include
> tennis, pony rides, puppet theaters, and toy sailboat rental
> (children float them in the large central fountain). Visitors

can also stop inside the Palais and attend a hearing of the French Senate, which is open to the public…

"Some of the Garden's more notable features include the Medici Fountain, erected in 1861, and a bronze replica of the Statue of Liberty. The park, which closes at sunset, also has a multitude of strolling paths, and is filled with hundreds of movable chairs, which can be rented. Outdoor concerts also occur in the Luxembourg Garden.

"The design is basically formal: a central parterre dominated by terraces. Alleés of trees surround the central terraces and continue in every direction except north, where the Palais du Luxembourg dominates. A free, more English-style garden is situated along Rue Guynemer and Rue Auguste-Comte; it was built during the first Empire and contains winding paths, grassy open areas, and a wide array of sculpture."

There's more about the *Jardin*'s history, and a great slide show, on PPS's website.

There's also an eloquent passage by David Whitley quoted in Terry Sisk's *Travel With Terry* website. Here's part of it:

"That it is called a garden rather than a park is a deliberate statement, the emphasis being on magnificent floral displays rather than vast expanses of lawn. The octagonal pool is surrounded by pots filled with vivid blooms which could pierce through the grayest of days. It's a scene to make you fall in love with the city instantly, particularly when you start looking at the detail…

"Just to wander from sector to sector, swigging from a bottle of water, is a delightfully affirmative experience. It's like a scene from 50 years ago, done up with modern costumes, and for the people-watcher, there's just so much to see. So many people, so many activities, so many expressions…

It's magical in the most simplistic way, and if you can't fall under the charm of Paris here, watching happy children rubbing the manes of their donkeys as they ride around the premises, then heaven help."

I can't say it better than that.

# 7.

# There Can Be So Much in a Name—or Not

"Town Square" in Las Vegas *(photo courtesy of PetLver/HART)*

To say that I am finicky about words is quite the understatement. I actually think there is a distinction to be made between "lend," the verb, and "loan," best used as a noun. I believe the English-speaking world would communicate more clearly if the subjunctive mood were still in widespread use; tragically, I suspect few readers under 40 even know that there is such a thing. Don't get me started on the difference between "that" and "which." As you might imagine, the language of marketing drives me crazy, and this applies to the marketing of places as well as that of goods and services. This story dissects an example.

Let's begin with some context: over a weekend not long ago I went to a birthday party for a smart and fun 13-year-old in my extended family, with three other kids and three other grownups. The upbeat restaurant was terrific for the occasion, and the company was swell. I had an excellent time, and it took my mind off of an impending return to work after a longish vacation.

The only fly in the ointment, so to speak, was the 60-mile drive, round-trip, from our house in the city out to the restaurant in the far suburbs. I wasn't about to complain, though, because for one thing it isn't a very nice thing to do; and, for another, absolutely nothing about a long drive to a kids' event would have seemed remarkable in the least to my adult companions, who are deeply committed suburbanites. For them, it's just part of ordinary daily life, like waking up and having breakfast. Walking or taking transit to an event, now *that* would have been remarkable.

The restaurant was at a place called Dulles Town Center. (Most readers probably recognize Dulles as the name of the large international airport in northern Virginia that serves the Washington, DC region; it is named for John Foster Dulles, a former Secretary of State.) To get there we went out the Dulles Toll Road that extends from the Capital Beltway and then Virginia Route 28. We took an exit, approached a road named City Center Boulevard, and pulled into a parking space near the restaurant.

The names Dulles Town Center and City Center Boulevard struck me as wildly ironic, if sadly familiar: where we were, there is no town; there is no center; there is no real boulevard; and there is certainly no city. What is actually there comprises hundreds of acres of low-rise sprawl, giant parking lots, arterial roads with scary 70-mph traffic, and 1.4 million square feet of shopping space in an enclosed mall. It is the mall, of course, that is named Dulles Town Center.

I'm not kidding when I say there is no town. There is a county (Loudoun, for some time one of America's fastest-growing), and then a bureaucratic artifice called a "census-designated place" that in this case apparently takes its name from the shopping mall. Sprawl may be dying at last, at least in its most egregious forms, but this excursion was a wake-up reminder that it's not dead yet.

I'm not saying, by the way, that the ironically named "Town Center" is a terrible place, once you're there. I get a little disoriented and freaked out when enclosed in huge shopping spaces, but I still would probably use this one if I lived out there. It certainly has stores that I patronize in other locations.

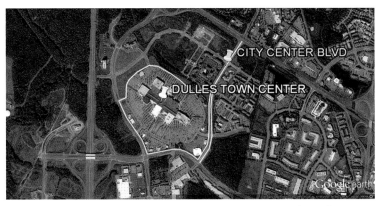

Dulles Town Center and City Center Boulevard *(image via Google Earth)*

But the whole thing got me thinking about the names that developers and marketers give to new places, frequently to evoke exactly what those places are not—or, worse, what they are no longer. We all know subdivisions with names like King Farm that replaced the actual King Farm, for example, or The Meadows where pavement has replaced the actual meadows.

I floated the idea for this story with friends, and Brenda volunteered that there is a big newish development called "Dunfarmin" near one of her bicycle routes in Maryland. No doubt. Jan reported that the joke near her home in North Carolina is that a subdivision called "Fox Run" is a reference to the one fox left who is running as fast as he can to get out of there.

I did a little internet research on the subject of naming new places and found plenty. One site, for example, reports a Saddle Ridge with no horses, a Paradise Park with no park, a Three Rivers Crossing miles from the nearest river, and a Canyon Lakes built on a dry hill. Another riffs on street names, reporting a Crabapple Lane linking two grim industrial parks, and a plot of McMansions where the streets are named Great Muskrat, Wooded Bog, Wild Turkey, and Nesting Duck. When I was researching NRDC's 1999 book *Once There Were Greenfields*, I came across a large if mundane development in Colorado where Spotted Owl Avenue intersects Wildcat Reserve Parkway (which, surprise, is not even a true parkway but just a wide road that links subdivisions to each other).

I found a real estate blog reporting that researchers from the University of Georgia "analyzed MLS Sales Data in Baton Rouge, Louisiana between 1984 and 2005 and found that buyers were willing to pay a premium of 4.2 percent for a property with 'country' in the name and an additional 5.1 percent for the phrase 'country club'."

Perhaps with that sort of thing in mind, several years ago Ken from the *DenverInfill* blog constructed a do-it-yourself template for naming subdivisions around Denver. Just choose one from each column, e.g., The [Plantation] at [Pine] [Gate] [Knoll]." There are also sites that will do the naming for you. I clicked on one site's random name generator and got "Wuthering Thicket North." I also asked the tongue-in-cheek "Real Estate Subdivision Name Generator" to produce five suggestions. Here are the results:

- Azalea Estates
- Breezy Highlands
- Fairford Overlook
- Magnolia Parish
- Breadfruit Inlet

You gotta love that last one. If you're in a particularly subversive mood, you can ask the word machine to generate negative names:

- Scavenger Swamp
- Buzzard Bog
- Fetid Bottoms
- Smelly Gully
- Monsoon Depression

Fun, no? Now, back to "town center." We actually do have some places in the DC suburbs that use but don't abuse the phrase, at least not to such an extent. Not all that far away from my relative's birthday party, for example, is Reston Town Center, a successful and praiseworthy attempt to create a walkable downtown for the suburb of Reston. Across the Potomac River in the Maryland 'burbs is Rockville Town Center, which, after some fits and starts, now also hosts a handsome, walkable, mixed-use environment.

Dulles Town Center *(image via Google Earth)*

And, in fact, Dulles Town Center may be headed in a similar direction. Erika Jacobson Moore wrote in the Loudoun Business section of the local news site *Leesburg Today* that the mall's owner has proposed to build over 1,600 new multifamily homes and up to 5.5 million square feet of commercial space on land adjacent to the mall, along with a public park, "a mass transit facility," and a commuter parking lot. According to Jacobson Moore's article, a spokesperson for the developer put it this way:

> "Now it is a suburban style development. It is a relic of the past [DTC opened in 1999]. If you look at the sea of parking and the asphalt, we thought it would be better to have an integrated, alive facility."

As things stood when the article was written, county planners were apparently opposed to the idea and the commissioners apparently divided. The proposal probably points in the right direction, and likely will be approved in some fashion; but the scale seems awfully ambitious to me given the dismal state of the real estate economy. I wouldn't expect much change anytime soon.

Meanwhile, the name of the short road that links the site's City Center Boulevard to the Town Center itself? "Mirage Way."

## More about Shopping Malls

### The Emptiest Mall in the World

The era of the giant enclosed shopping mall is coming to an end in America. Yes, plenty are still doing good business, even if Dulles Town Center's developer now calls it "a relic of the past." The key is that virtually no new malls are being built as older ones become outdated; the retail world has moved on to something closer to real town centers, if still not quite the same. There is now even a website, *deadmalls.com*, on which one can learn all about these changes and purchase "dead malls merchandise."

It is likely that no American mall, however, will ever be as empty and as dead as the world's largest, the New South China Mall in Dongguan, China. It is twice as big as the huge Mall of America outside Minneapolis. And it isn't just dying; it has never lived, having been nothing but empty since it opened seven years ago. According to its *Wikipedia* entry, it has an astounding 2,350 available retail spaces, 99 percent unoccupied.

Photographer and writer Matthew Niederhauser describes the mall on his eponymous blog:

> "A local billionaire built it, and they did not come. The South China Mall was the most ambitious and largest retail space ever conceived in China, if not the world, when it opened in 2005. Constructed smack in the middle of the Pearl River Delta between Shenzhen and Guangzhou, about 4 million people live within six miles of it, 9 million within

twelve miles and 40 million within sixty miles. Nonetheless, six years later, the South China Mall only maintains a 1 percent occupancy rate at best.

New South China Mall *(public domain photo)*

"This unabatedly empty temple to consumerism remains unfinished on top floors and is only sporadically visited thanks to the attached amusement park, Amazing World. For the time being dust and dismembered mannequins reign over the 6.5 million square foot venture. Although China might be the fastest growing consumer market in the world, the South China Mall reveals the vulnerability of this burgeoning economic giant."

The mall has 7,100,000 square feet (163 acres) of leasable floor space and 9,600,000 square feet (220 acres) of total space. *Wikipedia* reports that "the mall has seven zones modeled on international cities, nations and regions, including Amsterdam, Paris, Rome, Venice, Egypt, the Caribbean, and California." It has a replica of the Arc de

Triomphe, another of the bell tower of St. Mark's in Venice, and a 1.3-mile canal with gondolas.

What the New South China Mall (the owners added "new" to the name two years after the opening) doesn't have is people or business.

# 8.

# Sustainability Requires Attention to Legacy

Providence, Rhode Island *(photo by F. Kaid Benfield)*

Communities that hold on to the best of their past are demonstrating their sustainability in a very literal way. It's almost a tautology, isn't it? I believe preserving important aspects of older buildings and communities matters a great deal, both because doing so is good green stewardship and because knowing our legacy is a foundation of knowing our communities—and ourselves—today.

Preservationist Carl Elefante is credited with the wonderful phrase, "the greenest building is the one that is already built." There is much truth in that statement.

Indeed, older buildings and neighborhoods have intrinsic green properties such as embodied energy and resources (as discussed in Chapter 3) and, frequently, "original green" characteristics such as climate-specific design common before what my friend and architectural thought leader Steve Mouzon calls "The Thermostat Age." Older properties also serve a less measurable, but no less important, function in constituting a shared cultural legacy. Simply put, they remind us where we—and our places—came from. They keep every place from looking and feeling like every other place, no easy task in today's mass-market economy.

A city's chances for lasting success will be enhanced when it (1) recognizes its historic assets; (2) builds upon those assets by courting the kinds of businesses and residents that appreciate their unique character; and (3) preserves those assets for the future, with appropriate law, policy, and practice.

Allow me to get a bit mushy about this: When we think of "sustainability," we are usually considering the viability of a place or action into the future—as Steve Mouzon puts it, "can we keep it going in a healthy way into an uncertain future?" But I increasingly think that, when we consider that nourishing the human spirit is just as important to people habitat as conserving natural resources—we also must consider the past: we must understand what, exactly, we seek to sustain.

On a bike ride not long ago, I stopped with my camera at Glen Echo Park, an old art deco amusement park just outside the city of Washington. It is now owned by the National Park Service and managed by a nonprofit organization as a historic site and creative center. It has a ballroom, a theater, an arcade (now galleries), a former bumper car pavilion that now serves as a music venue (go back a couple of decades and you might have heard my band play there), and the star of the show, a still-functioning carousel. There are also refreshments, plenty of trees, and picnic tables. It's not an urban environment *per se*, but it's the kind of place that provides nearby respite—and, dare I say, joy—to counter the intensity of city living.

Kids love the place, as you might imagine. There is plenty for them to do, in a great atmosphere. And I can't help but wonder whether part of Glen Echo's magic is that it is not, at least not now, a fully functioning amusement park but mostly an evocation of one. Very little is spoon-fed to its visitors, who must instead engage the place with their own imaginations. And that, perhaps, is exactly what preservation at its best does for all of us.

Glen Echo Park *(photo by F. Kaid Benfield)*

For me, the feeling is not exactly nostalgia, since I never knew Glen Echo when it was fully functioning, nor did I know any amusement park quite like it. But I get it that places like Glen Echo are part of our shared legacy. I'm connected to it culturally if not personally. I feel comfortable there in a way that I wouldn't if I were in a new replica of it or in a modern-day amusement park.

At the park's entrance, for a long time there was also—somewhat sadly—an old, deteriorating trolley car and a segment of track from back when trolleys were Washington's primary mode of public transportation. The park was the last stop on the line and, I'm told, Washingtonians would head out there after work on summer evenings. (Speaking of transportation, on my bike ride, my comfort with Glen Echo also had something to do with a well-placed break at mile 23 or so of a 31-mile ride in which I had been pushing the pace.)

Also sadly, Glen Echo's rich history included segregation: it was whites-only for 63 out of its fully operational 70 years. Ugh. Its cultural legacy is obviously very different for African-Americans than for whites. But perhaps important nonetheless. The park opened to all, finally, in 1961.

Glen Echo Park *(photo by F. Kaid Benfield)*

I find Glen Echo especially evocative in late fall, when the crowds are gone and the leaves are down, opening up the views. The carousel is closed for the season. There is less going on that engages me on its own terms, and more for me to relate to in my own ways.

Why is this important? Another friend, Chuck Wolfe, wrote an essay about "reclaiming the urban memory":

> "A simultaneous, street-based nostalgia targets simpler times, a more human scale and an elusive world of accessible neighborhoods often lost in the memories of previous generations. Consider imagery which restores such lost urban memories for those who did not witness modern urban history, and recreates what political writer Alexander Cockburn has termed 'the lost valleys of the imagination.'"

I suppose Glen Echo supplies that lost memory for me, since I never experienced anything quite like it when it was viable as an amusement park.

Ultimately, our responsibility toward legacy is not just about cultural legacy but also about stewardship. And I would submit that we must be good stewards not just of historic buildings and neighborhoods but also of their contexts. To rephrase Elefante's dictum, the greenest building will not be the one that's already built if it has been abandoned, and rendered nonfunctional and deteriorating because its community or neighborhood has been disinvested. I have long thought that the greatest contribution that the National Trust's visionary former president, Dick Moe, made to the cause was to understand that the flight of people and resources from older communities to new subdivisions and malls on the suburban fringe was antithetical to saving older buildings and historic neighborhoods. He believed it was in the interest of preservationists to fight sprawl and support revitalization, and I do, too.

Crown Square, St. Louis, before restoration *(photo courtesy of Old North Restoration Group)*

This means that preservation—particularly green preservation—requires thinking about how we want our metro areas to be shaped as we go into the future. Will our development patterns be supportive of older communities and neighborhoods? Is the historic asset that we wish to preserve in a strong, supportive neighborhood context? Good, sustained stewardship of our built-environment legacy requires that the answer to both questions must be yes.

If, as I believe, pursuing sustainability requires choosing what to sustain, then doing so with wisdom requires access to the past and attention to context. And it requires engaging our imaginations, our spiritual as well as our scientific sides. As perhaps only my musical hero Van Morrison might put it, in his majestic "The Beauty of the Days Gone By," one regards the past "to contemplate my own true self, and keep me young as I grow old."

## More about Legacy

### We Must Be Discerning about What We Preserve

Preservationists know instinctively the importance of connecting to the past and maintaining a legacy as we go forward. But the integration of the past into the present and future is the hard part. How much do we save and what do we do with it? What do we preserve as is, what do we alter and/or adapt, and what do we allow to be demolished?

Aging supermarket in my neighborhood, 2011 *(photo via Google Earth)*

I believe that preservationists must be discriminating and wise in asserting our values, in order to maintain the continued support of the public. If we always push our principles to the maximum without awareness of the consequences to other important societal values, we risk losing our credibility, among other things.

More specifically, every building that is 50 years old—the minimum age traditionally required for designation as a historic landmark—is not worthy of legal protection. Within walking distance of my house, for example, some people tried to block a great development—a mid-rise collection of attractive buildings and plazas that would finally give the neighborhood a sense of place—by asserting that the ugly, plain, dysfunctional old supermarket on the site was historically significant. They didn't care about the building at all. They wanted it replaced, actually, just not with what was proposed. So they played the historic preservation card, in my opinion damaging the reputation of a movement that needs to be taken seriously when the property in question is truly worthy. (Their petition was eventually withdrawn and, after a thirteen-year delay resolved by litigation, the new development is finally being built.) I believe those of us who care about the built environment must be discerning in asserting our cause and vigilant against those who hurt us by abusing it.

The problem is not limited to those who invoke the good name of preservation to pursue more selfish aims. I also think that, at least with regard to neighborhood defensiveness in response to development activities, we in the environmental movement have played a big role. For good reasons, beginning in the 1970s we created a system of laws and procedures, and a culture that, over time, has made it relatively easy to challenge proposed development of all types, and to defeat proposals or delay them until proponents give up. People now consider it their right to fight proposed development wherever and whenever it occurs, and resistance to change has become an expectation in many places.

While there are important reasons to be glad for our legal protections—many, many bad projects have been halted because of environmental challenges, some of them litigated by yours truly—I think that, as the creators of this system, we now bear some responsibility for making sure that it is not abused. Heaven knows, given the decades of bad development that have been forced upon a mostly helpless public, it is understandable for folks to be distrustful of change. But it is time for us as a movement to become more discriminating in what we challenge and what we applaud, to speak more publicly and forcefully for things as well as against things, and to challenge those who oppose environmentally benign or beneficial projects in our name.

# 9.

# But the Past Is Not the Future

Thanksgiving 1870 by Edw. Ridley & Sons Co., New York City *(public domain)*

While I believe strongly that paying attention to legacy in our built environment is important both to sustainability and to our self-awareness, we should not make the mistake of confusing legacy with demographics. The society of tomorrow—and the environment required to support it—will be fundamentally different from that of yesterday or even today. I began this essay on the day before Thanksgiving, as I was contemplating a gathering of extended family on this most familial of holidays.

We romanticize family in our society: just watch TV commercials for confirmation. But does our idealized version of family life resemble real family life? Does it exclude people who are not part of or close to their families? Is the concept of "family" changing, with implications for the built environment? The answers are, of course, seldom; usually; and definitely.

Why does this matter to communities and sustainability? Because we must plan the future of our cities and neighborhoods to account for reality, not our memories, or a rosy version of what some believe today's households "should" be, or even our own personal situations.

As it turns out, the way households are going to be evolving over the next few decades is toward more singles, empty-nesters, and city-lovers, none of whom particularly want the big yards and long commutes they may have grown up with as kids. A significant market for those things will still exist, but it will be a smaller portion of overall housing demand than it used to be. This new reality means that the communities and businesses that take account of these emerging preferences for smaller homes and lots and more walkable neighborhoods will be the ones that are most successful.

## The Great Convergence

My friend Laurie Volk, a market analyst of considerable wisdom and repute, says that a major underlying reason for these market shifts is the "great convergence," as she calls it, of the two largest generations in American history. Together the Baby Boomers (born roughly 1946-1964) and Millennials (sometimes called Generation Y born roughly born 1981-2000), account for more than 150 million Americans, a little less than half of the total. Today, neither the city-oriented Millennials nor the empty-nesting Boomers fit into the traditional suburban housing market to nearly the same degree as the Boomers did a few decades ago, when they were raising kids and the kids hadn't yet become the Millennials.

In the 1960s and 1970s, fully half of American households were couples with kids. That portion is already down to a third and headed to become only a quarter of the total.

Yet the current mixture of housing types on the ground—especially that built within the pre-recession time frame of from 1975 to 2005 or so—doesn't come anywhere close to matching the more current preference for walkable, mixed-use neighborhoods. Wonder no more why city living is becoming more expensive.

Indeed, real estate analyst extraordinaire Arthur C. (Chris) Nelson was telling us as long ago as 2005 that, because of changing demographics and consumer preferences, the supply of large-lot suburban housing was already overbuilt in comparison to future demand. As a result, Nelson predicted that the value of large-lot properties was going to decline to less than their amount of mortgage debt, a circumstance now known as "under water." Experience has proven his analysis to be right on target: although large-lot suburban homes weren't the only ones that went into heavy debt and foreclosure during The Great Recession, there's no doubt that they were hit the worst.

I performed my own analysis of several data sets of real estate price changes in the metropolitan Washington, DC region over the past six years. There is a clear geographic pattern to the degree of change, with homes in the outer suburbs suffering the greatest percentage losses in value and the slowest rates of recovery. Median home sales prices in the inner city and adjacent close suburbs actually

With one exception, inner locations lead the area's housing recovery
*(image by F. Kaid Benfield via Google Earth)*

increased in some cases at the same time as those on the fringe were suffering losses of 25 percent or worse.

In fact, we now have examples where farmland that was sold for real estate speculation is now being sold again, back to farming investors who seek to return the land to crop production. If that doesn't tell us enough about the shifts in the market for exurban housing, then consider the relative demise of the McMansion era of neo-trophy houses, their popularity now only a small fraction of what it once was.

There may be another market shift afoot, too: from a housing market dominated by owner-occupied properties to one with a higher share of rentals. Ben Brown of the small but highly respected planning and development advisory group Placemakers fears that in some ways our neighborhoods aren't ready for more rentals:

> "The problem is, outside of big city downtowns, where demand for rentals has always been high, the design and construction of apartments, town houses and other rental models hasn't consistently measured up to the range and standards of single-family, for sale residences. In too many places, 'for rent' and 'affordable' have become code words for subsidized government housing or cheaply built complexes likely to be opposed by neighbors worried about their property values or the increased traffic congestion. There's a stigma to overcome…

> "The ideal approach would be to produce neighborhood-appropriate rental choices that are impossible to tell from for-sale dwellings. Historic in-town neighborhoods provide the best models. True townhouses. Appropriately scaled stacked flats. And, of course, single-family detached homes that toggle between owner-occupied and rented depending upon market conditions and owner preferences."

If the market for rentals does indeed strengthen, perhaps the quality will pick up as Brown suggests it should.

More generally, since market forces usually do respond to changes in demand, we can probably expect to continue to see more urban and walkable suburban housing types built on currently vacant and underutilized properties. The question is how quickly the change will occur.

## What the Census Says about the Modern American Household

In 2012 the Census Bureau released some fascinating statistics about the state of American households. People are marrying later than they used to, for example, if they marry at all. This is one of the reasons why the number and portion of people living alone has risen steadily and significantly for decades.

The portion of children living with two parents has dropped dramatically from 1960, from just under 90 percent of all children in 1960 to around 70 percent in 2012. Statistically, almost all of the change can be explained by a dramatic increase in the portion of children living with single moms. (But it's not for the old reasons: the percentage of kids living with widowed, separated, and divorced mothers has actually gone down in recent decades. There has been a sharp increase, however, in the portion living with never-married mothers.)

In general, married-couple households have declined sharply since the 1950s, from over 75 percent of all households then to about 50 percent now. The major share of that change has been an increase in "nonfamily households" consisting of singles or persons not "related to each other by birth, marriage or adoption." Average household size has gone down, too, from about 3.7 persons in 1940 to about 2.6 persons now; family households have dropped from about 3.8 persons to about 3.1. (It says much about our consumptive society that, until very recently, the size of the average new home in America has been increasing dramatically even while household size has been declining.)

For a slim majority (52 percent) of married couples, both spouses are in the labor force. But the portion fitting the 1950s "traditional" model where the husband works and the wife doesn't is much smaller (about 23 percent). In the remainder of married households, either

the wife works and the husband doesn't, or neither works. There has
been a steady decrease in the portion of households where only the
husband works since at least the 1980s.

Even for couples with kids under six years old, a majority of
households have both spouses in the labor force. But, for married
couples with kids under 15, about a quarter have stay-at-home mothers, consistent with the related statistic above.

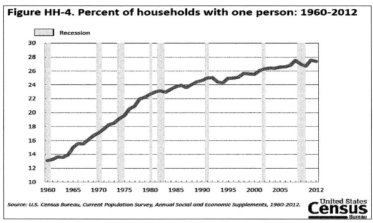

Growth in one-person households *(image by US Census Bureau)*

What I take from all these data is that there really is no "typical" American family living under the same roof these days, if there
ever was. Rather, we have a diverse and changing array of household
types and circumstances that smart planners, builders, and businesses
will seek to accommodate. The census data show that the growing
parts of the housing market are nonfamily households, smaller households including people living alone, unmarried couples, single-parent
households with kids, and older households. The declining parts of
the market are larger families, married couples, two-parent households, and couples with only one breadwinner, though each of these
categories clings to a significant share of the total.

In other words, just as Volk's analysis of "the great convergence"
of generations and Nelson's analysis of current supply and demand
trends suggest, the portion of households that is decreasing the most
is exactly that portion most likely to seek homes in large-lot, outer

suburbs. Look for continued lower prices in that market and continued high prices in the urban and walkable suburban markets until supply catches up to demand.

## Looking to the Future

Forecasters inside the real estate industry agree. A report on the future of housing from The Demand Institute, a think tank that tracks consumer demand, also came out in 2012. Among the findings that are promising for more sustainable development patterns is the assertion that the strongest segment of today's housing market "comprises populous urban or semi-urban communities well served by local amenities." In the report, *The Shifting Nature of US Housing Demand*, the authors call this segment the "resilient walkables" and forecast a home price rise of up to five percent per year in this segment between 2014 and 2017.

The analysis confirms that the weakest segment of the market, by contrast, is located in outer and smaller suburbs or outlying areas that "are sparsely populated, and have low walkability." Though prices for this segment are "relatively cheap," the authors contend that the value of these "weighed down" properties will not increase enough to reach the national average even by 2017.

In other words, if you're a real estate investor, put your money on smart growth and avoid sprawl. A closer read of the new report, however, contains a lot of nuances, mostly but not entirely consistent with what other analysts such as Volk and Nelson have been saying with regard to growing demand for walkable neighborhoods. From the report:

- Nationally, the housing recovery will accelerate between 2015 and 2017.
- The recovery will be led by increasing demand for rental homes, especially from younger people and immigrants. The national share of occupied rental homes as a portion of the total rose from 31 percent in 2005 to 35 percent in 2012, and home ownership has declined sharply among persons under 35. "The only segment of the home building

sector now showing clear signs of recovery is multifamily housing," driven by developers seeking to rent.

- But the dominance in rentals may be temporary. Conversion of for-sale homes now in oversupply to rentals will clear the excess, the authors say, after which home ownership will rise and return to historical levels.

- After increasing steadily for decades, the average size of the American home has begun to shrink and will continue to do so. By 2015, average new home size should be back to where it was in the mid-1990s.

- The extent to which walkability helps the market may depend on where you are. In addition to the strong "resilient walkable" category and the weak "weighed down" category, the report identifies two other segments: "slow but steady" homes in areas with average walkability and employment rates; and a "damaged but hopeful" segment, where neighborhoods are highly walkable but suffer from a weak regional economy. Both will see price recovery, though not as quickly and strongly as the resilient walkables; the slow but steady group will see it sooner than the damaged but hopeful group.

- In a prediction I find troubling, the report says that "neighborhoods will be increasingly segregated economically, resulting in polarization." The authors observe that the portion of Americans living in middle-income neighborhoods has declined considerably in recent decades, while the portions living in both affluent and poor neighborhoods has increased. "Housing stock within neighborhoods will become more homogeneous."

- While the increased demand for urban and walkable, transit-served neighborhoods is clear—the authors note the positive correlation between prices and walkability, as measured by the popular website Walk Score—"many Americans, particularly those planning to purchase, will move even farther from the city to suburbs where housing is more affordable." (The report does not delve into the effect that energy prices may have on that movement.)

- Increased demand for urban, smaller, and rental properties will produce ancillary effects. Industries that will do well include home remodeling, carsharing, and portable appliances. Homes with less space for storage but more accessibility to shops may also lead consumers to more frequent purchases of smaller sizes of packaged goods.

So, particularly for those of us who seek a future of more mixed-income neighborhoods with a variety of housing types, we should pay attention to policy shifts that can help us get there, since this forecast suggests that the market alone may be helpful but not sufficient to accomplish the goal. The report also suggests that maintaining a supply of affordable for-sale units in high-demand walkable neighborhoods may be critical to dampening a potential rebound market for sprawl.

Still, after decades of both policy and market forces wreaking damage on central cities while paving over cornfields and forests to build mediocre development, the central finding is heartening:

> "Although demand for new and existing homes will rise, consumer demographics as well as altered preferences will change the nature of that demand...demand will be high in areas well served with amenities that are within walking distance and that have a sense of community. Sprawling, featureless suburbs will be less attractive."

The more cities and inner suburbs strengthen, the more the environment will benefit.

## More about the Future

### What Will Technology and Changes in Workplace Practices Mean for Cities?

I attended a meeting in Washington at which a prominent smart growth leader was showing a presentation on "the business case for smart growth." Much of it was based on the need for everyday, face-to-face business communication within companies and the need for dense environments to facilitate efficient productivity and movement of goods. He stressed that this has always been the case, making connections to history and to studies reaching back for decades.

There was only one problem. Several meeting attendees were participating via conference call, following along via their computers and internet connections in remote locations. They were virtually countering the speaker's point as he was making it.

Indeed, a number of participants in the meeting were environmental and urbanist organizations who were, and are, advocating telecommuting as a way of saving transportation energy and infrastructure. Transportation for America, a coalition with a staff based in Washington, DC, has a communications director who works remotely from Seattle. A prominent staff member at DC-based Smart Growth America works from Montana. An official at the US Patent and Trademark Office, which has an aggressive telecommuting program, reports that up to a staggering 80 percent of agency employees might be working from remote locations at any given moment. Heck, I have one colleague who worked seamlessly for NRDC (in theory, as an employee of our San Francisco office) from Italy for five years, for no other reason than because she wanted to and could make it work. And so on.

The modern workplace
*(photo courtesy of rxb/Richard)*

Our speaker was making a twentieth-century argument in a twenty-first-century economy.

And yet the twenty-first century is shaping up as a decidedly urban epoch, with downtowns more popular than they have been in 50 years and suburbs reshaping themselves in ever-more urban forms. What's going on?

Thomas Fisher, dean of the College of Design at the University of Minnesota, believes that we are undergoing an enormous change in "how people will live and work, in how businesses will operate, and in what services and support we will need from government." Writing in *The Huffington Post*, Fisher contends that the 20th-century model of large-scale, heavy industry is largely over and that the new workforce is much more independent and nimble:

> "In the next economy, 'manufacturing' may more-often occur at a micro scale, with free-lancers 3D printing in their back bedroom or the self-employed laser-cutting products in their garage…Self-employed entrepreneurs rely upon durable, high-bandwidth infrastructure in order to communicate with and ship to customers globally. They need affordable health care equivalent to what large companies provide their employees. And they tend to congregate in places with a high quality of life, where other entrepreneurs go."

So, yes, we still want to congregate, maybe more than we have in a long time, but for different reasons now.

Continuing, Fisher explains that the new economy demands changes in our built environment, to encourage the use of old buildings in new ways and to foster intermingled homes, workplaces, and shops:

> "With the rise of the contingent workforce, people will also live and work in ways we haven't seen for a very long time. We have developed our cities based on the old economy, with residential, commercial, and industrial areas kept separate and 'pure' through single-use zoning. That made

sense in an economy that divided our work lives from our private lives, and that spawned large-scale noxious industries that no one wanted nearby. The next economy, though, may look more like the way in which people lived and worked prior to the industrial revolution, in which home, office, and shop co-exist in some combination of physical and digital space. This may require rethinking our zoning laws to allow for a much finer-grain mix of uses and repurposing buildings designed for single functions that will have no tenants or buyers if they remain that way."

With former retail mainstays such as bookstores and music stores giving way to digital commerce—and workplaces getting smaller—we'll still need urban neighborhoods, mainly for "what we can't get any other way." This will certainly include face-to-face conversation, not necessarily for traditional business reasons but for socializing and for impromptu idea generation among entrepreneurs. And we may need a new educational approach, too—one that stresses creativity, since preparing students for an ordered world that is becoming less so every day could be a disservice.

These new realities, of course, lead directly to urban thinker Richard Florida's argument that we need cities more than ever, not to maximize efficiencies in the old order but to nourish the creativity required for success in the new. He elaborates in *Business Insider*:

> "Cities are veritable magnetrons for creativity. Great thinkers, artists, and entrepreneurs—the Creative Class writ large—have always clustered and concentrated in cities. Deeper in our past the concentration of people in cities not only powered advances in agriculture, but led to the basic innovations in tool-making and the rudimentary arts that came to define civilization...

> "Real cities have real neighborhoods. They are filled with the flexible old buildings that are ideal for incubating new ideas. They are made up of mixed use, pedestrian scale

neighborhoods that literally push people out into the street, cafes and other third places, encouraging the serendipitous interactions, the constant combinations and recombinations that result in new ideas, new businesses and new industries."

So, in the end, the speaker who was making the "business case for smart growth" was right that modern businesspeople need urban environments, but perhaps not for the traditional reasons he was citing. If the reasons matter—and Fisher and Florida certainly suggest that they do—both city planners and companies should take note to ensure that they are prepared for new ways of living and conducting business. Cities will still be cities, but education, retail, and workplaces may all need to change, along with government services and regulation. The companies and communities that figure this out first are likely to be the ones that succeed best in the next economy. Likewise for urban advocates.

# 10.

# Community Isn't What It Used to Be, Apparently

Day care at Wisconsin Avenue Baptist Church, Washington, DC *(photo by F. Kaid Benfield)*

The extent to which our perceptions and bonds of community have been changing was milling around in my head for a long time before I decided to write about it. What finally prompted me was a ferocious battle in my neighborhood challenging a proposed addition, modest in size, to a Baptist church's building. The addition would house a nonprofit child care center, a language school for kids, and the Washington Conservatory of Music, which the church hosts. To me, it seemed just the sort of thing we would want in our neighborhood. But not to others, obviously, which led me to think about the nature of "community."

Some neighbors said that the small addition to the Wisconsin Avenue Baptist Church wouldn't be the end of it. They complained that the church had also hosted all sorts of other nefarious activities, such as meetings of Overeaters Anonymous, summer camps, a girls' chorus, the City Choir of Washington, and even a program for "troubled youth," according to a quote in the neighborhood newspaper. Geez, what next, the neighbors must have wondered? Pot-luck suppers? Musical classes for the homeless? The traffic and people were already unbearable, went the argument.

Maybe it's just me, but these activities sounded—and still sound—like the sorts of things that churches have always done, and our communities are better because of them. I can't imagine neighbors raising this kind of ruckus in my youth. (And I'm glad, since my band used to rehearse in our church's social hall and host musical performances there.) If it meant a little more traffic or whatever, that was okay, because our community was proud of this stuff.

In any event, in this case the dreaded traffic never came, even though the church addition was, in fact, built. I walk, ride my bike, and drive by it all the time, at all hours of the day, and now, five years since construction was completed, I have yet to see anything remotely approaching the "constant stream of traffic" cited by the complainants. In fact, there is hardly ever *any* significant traffic, by city standards.

The same neighborhood paper that reported the controversy over the Baptist church also ran an article around the same time about a nearby neighborhood's "victory" over an evangelical church, preventing a movie theater from following through on its plans to host the church's Sunday morning services. "Some residents worried about the traffic and parking problems," reported the paper. (Wouldn't the theater's usual movies present the same issues?) And others, well, they just didn't like the kind of church it was. They fought the plan on zoning grounds and eventually the theater withdrew its proposal.

Again, the contrast with the way communities used to operate is striking. When I was a child, my parents belonged to a congregation that didn't yet have a building. We met for services on Sunday mornings at a local elementary school until the church was built. Again, no big deal. Today, maybe evolving sensitivities about separation of church and state would question whether public school use for religious activities is appropriate, but I can assure you that back in the day it also would not have been a problem to house the services in a private building such as a commercial movie theater.

In the DC case, it especially troubles me that the objection to the proposed services was tinged with apparent disdain for the evangelical nature of the religion in question. Somehow I don't think there would have been such strong objection if the theater had proposed, say, children's matinees on Sunday mornings instead of evangelical church services. Although I'm no evangelical, that rubs me the wrong way.

Yet another vigorous neighborhood fight broke out in a different part of town over a proposed two-story Mormon church on a street that already has 45 existing churches. The 46th, opponents said, would be out of character with the neighborhood. (Okay, the steeple—cited by the opponents—is higher than even I would prefer, but it's still quite a bit shorter than the steeple on the church that my friends Bob and Barbara attend, on the same street a mile to the south.) And in yet another part of town, neighbors challenged the permit for a Buddhist center on Massachusetts Avenue, a street well-known for its embassies, churches, and other institutional buildings, on the grounds that the facility was not a "house of worship" under the law. (They lost.)

It's not just churches that are drawing citizens' fire: it's schools, too. A neighborhood in suburban Virginia waged a passionate fight over expansion of a Montessori school. (Talk about a menace to society.) And the DC neighborhood just south of mine had a protracted, bitter fight over the National Cathedral School's new athletic facility, even though it was mostly built underground. "Oppose the Coliseum—Don't Throw the Neighborhood to the Lions!" shouted the signs in neighborhood yards. (The National Cathedral School is operated by the Episcopal Church, and serves girls in grades 4-12. It is on the grounds of Washington National Cathedral, a 57-acre site, only 14 percent of which may be developed.)

National Cathedral School, Washington, DC *(photo by F. Kaid Benfield)*

Do you see a coliseum in the photo of the NCS? See that green space? Green space that neighbors can use? (There's a lot more of it to the right of the photo.) That's the new gym's roof! That dispute went to court, the neighbors lost, and the gym was built. The neighborhood remains green and peaceful; traffic has not increased significantly; and property values have continued rising, despite the downturn in property values elsewhere.

I could go on and on. I could tell stories of neighborhoods opposing nursing homes—nursing homes! My favorite of all these DC battles, though, is the instance when a tony neighborhood refused to let a charity run pass through, because it would have required closing the street for *two hours* on a Sunday morning, once a year. I forget the charity, but I think it was medical—leukemia, maybe? The event had to be re-routed.

What the heck happened between my youth and now, to the point where what used to be regarded as community assets are now regarded as community threats? As my friend Merry wrote, "I've been thinking about this kind of thing a lot (neighborhoods and community, now vs. then) and feel like I am missing some key piece of the puzzle...as if I fell asleep for a few years (college & grad school?) and missed some major societal change that caused this." If we are experiencing hostility between neighbors and even our most basic community institutions, the viability of multi-functional, sustainable neighborhoods and cities is called into question.

While I don't believe that civic and religious institutions deserve a *carte blanche* to do anything they want without being questioned, I perceive a level of distrust and defensiveness in these cases that is out of proportion to the proposals. And, frankly, it seems most prevalent in upscale neighborhoods. I don't think it is a coincidence that some of the greatest community development success stories, sometimes supported by faith-based organizations, have occurred in recently downtrodden or relatively modest areas like Dudley Street in Boston, Old North in St. Louis, and Greensburg, Kansas.

I don't think it has always been this way. Are we as a society less communal and less trusting, more defensive than we used to be? If so, why?

I have a few theories. First, air conditioning. I'm serious. People can spend more time indoors comfortably than they could, say, 50 years ago, which means less interaction. How many people sit on their front porches in the evenings now, if they even have them, in upscale neighborhoods? Second, our addiction to automobiles. As my co-author Don Chen memorably wrote in our 1999 book *Once There Were Greenfields*, some people, particularly in low-density suburbs, "tend to interact with their neighbors mainly through their windshields." We no longer know each other in the way we used to.

And, of course, we're a more mobile society in general. Communities have more transient populations than they used to have, weakening the kinds of bonds that are forged over time by face-to-face interaction.

Whatever the reasons, there has been a decided downturn in Americans' affinity with both churches and schools. In his classic book *Bowling Alone: the Collapse and Revival of American Community*, Robert Putnam noted that, although the US continues to have more houses of worship per capita than any other nation on earth, "religious sentiment in America seems to be becoming somewhat less tied to institutions and more self-defined." Weekly churchgoing remains popular in the US but has declined over the last half-century, as has church membership.

Phoebe Hearst Elementary School, Washington, DC *(photo by F. Kaid Benfield)*

With respect to schools, Putnam observed that "participation in parent-teacher organizations has dropped drastically...from more than 12 million in 1964 to barely 5 million in 1982 before recovering to approximately 7 million" in 1995. Putnam also used survey data to document declining social contact with neighbors and the declining portion of the population who say that "most people can be trusted," which had fallen sharply to below 40 percent by the mid-1990s.

In my youth, neighbors were more accepting of modest development proposals by nearby churches and schools, I believe, because they were usually among those who attended them, or were friends with people who did. Today, given the decline in identification with these institutions, and decline in neighborhood social ties, neighbors see the local churches and schools not as their own but as the province of *other people*, at best representative of a minority in the neighborhood. They are much less inclined to give the benefit of the doubt.

Washington National Cathedral *(photo courtesy of NCinDC/Josh)*

To return the discussion back to my neighborhood, it is a long but immensely pleasant walk, about a mile, from my house to what is undoubtedly our neighborhood's greatest asset - Washington National Cathedral. The foundation stone was laid in 1907 and it took 83 years to build. No matter what your religious or social affinity, you'd be hard pressed not to find inspiration in its majesty. Renters and homebuyers pay a considerable premium for being located nearby, especially if their properties have a view. The cathedral, one of the world's largest, opens its doors to people of all faiths as they gather to worship and pray, to mourn the passing of world leaders, and to confront the pressing moral and social issues of the day. I can't imagine our city without it.

We are lucky that construction of the cathedral began a century ago. Would Washington National Cathedral be allowed in its neighborhood if it were proposed today?

# More about the Habit of Saying No

## A Personal Journey to Yes

As I discussed in another essay in the context of seeing cities as providing solutions to environmental challenges, the environmental movement was born on the premise of saying yes to wilderness and nature, but no to nearly any form of development. Finding a self-identified environmentalist who supported land development of any kind at the first Earth Day in 1970 would have been nearly impossible. But we now know that, although our "yes" was spot on, our "no" was too pervasive.

I began my professional career as a litigation lawyer (not in the environmental field, which barely existed when I graduated from law school) and it took me forever to shake the label. I was good at it. When I found my way to the Natural Resources Defense Council, it was as a litigator. I saved quite a bit of forest land from being needlessly logged, helped save the organization from a defamation suit (trust me: it's more fun being the plaintiff), and I'm proud of all that. But, after quite a few years, I came to realize that the world of arbitrary deadlines, constant jockeying for legal advantage with abstract arguments about procedure, and being adversarial for a living isn't for everyone, and it wasn't really for me. I was yearning to be a more solution-oriented advocate.

Fortunately, a few visionary leaders at NRDC were pointing to a new kind of environmentalism. My colleague (and future Heinz laureate) Ralph Cavanagh was blazing a new trail, figuring out a way for electric utilities to make more money from managing demand for electricity than by building or expanding power plants. My colleague (and future MacArthur laureate) David Goldstein was devising a way for mortgage lenders to make money by investing in "location-efficient" neighborhoods that required less driving and thus freed up borrowers' incomes to make homebuying more accessible.

NRDC's energy program became champions of a new wave of solutions recognizing that all business wasn't evil, that with the right programs we could become partners instead of adversaries. And with better results for the planet, frequently, than we were getting out of some of our litigation and lobbying. When our energy team was looking in the mid-1990s for someone to address transportation efficiency, I could not have been more ready.

It took about five minutes for me to discover that transportation efficiency was really about land use. And so were a lot of other environmental challenges, from conservation of the landscape to healthy waterways to clean air to wetlands preservation and more. But the "aha" solution for land use was still missing: sprawl was certainly the villain, but what could be the land use equivalent of Ralph's industry-friendly utilities reform?

I didn't really find the way until I read of uber-architect/planner/thinker Peter Calthorpe's work in articulating (and naming) "transit-oriented development," the now-familiar phrase for walkable communities built around neighborhood conveniences and public transportation stops, and until I read about equally uber-architect/planner/thinker Andres Duany's pioneering work in creating a non-sprawling community in Seaside, Florida. Their templates addressed land use and transportation at once, and made for convivial neighborhoods, too. Here was something positive to advocate. It was good for developers, good for residents, and great for the environment, compared to sprawl.

As I was soon to learn, I wasn't alone in my excitement. A growing group of us were arriving at the same conclusions at the same time. Elements of the solutions were being developed not just within architectural and planning circles but also at places like the Environmental Defense Fund, Center for Neighborhood Technology, the federal Environmental Protection Agency, state leaders within Oregon and Maryland, the Sierra Club, American Farmland Trust, Conservation Fund, Surface Transportation Policy Project, the National Trust for Historic Preservation, the Enterprise Foundation, Duany and Calthorpe's Congress for the New Urbanism, and more.

That was almost twenty years ago, and I haven't looked back. It would be a bad idea for both myself and my clients for me to resume litigating at this point, but I hope my litigator colleagues keep doggedly at their work; there are still far too many important environmental battles that need to be fought and won. Our "no," properly applied, remains critical in a world of excess. But I am also glad that the environmental movement has grown into a more complex and sophisticated organism, just as passionate about when to say yes as about when to say no.

# 11.

# Meet the Environmental Paradox of Smart Growth

San Francisco *(photo courtesy of Richard Masoner)*

A secret truth of smart growth is that it manages environmental impacts by concentrating them and, in some places, intensifying them. For example, if we absorb new growth by increasing development and the number of residents in city centers and around transit stations, research proves that the environmental impacts per increment of new growth on the region as a whole can be substantially less than if the growth is allowed to sprawl ever-outward. But, in the specific areas where growth and development are intensifying, we may also be increasing noise, traffic, and pollution. I call this "the paradox of smart growth" and believe that we serve our communities and our cause better if we acknowledge and mitigate it.

A s I argue throughout this book, to move more deliberately toward anything resembling a sustainable future, we need to use land more efficiently and build more compactly. We need higher densities of homes and businesses per acre than we built, on average, in the new development of the late 20th century. We especially must do this in two ways: (1) by retrofitting or "repairing" low-density suburbs, especially by taking advantage of redevelopment opportunities as aging commercial buildings go out of service, and (2) as I also argue throughout this book, by reinvesting and rebuilding in disinvested parts of central cities and older towns and suburbs. Those aren't the only circumstances in which we should accommodate more people, homes, and buildings than we may have now, but it would be a heck of a start.

The rewards are substantial: less pressure to develop rural lands; reduced rates of driving, and cleaner air through consequent reduced emissions; more walkable neighborhoods and more viable public transit; cleaner waterways through reduced spread of runoff-causing pavement around what are now well-functioning watersheds; increased tax revenues for cash-strapped local governments; and opportunities to apply design lessons so that we may create better places. That's a lot of benefit. While I am on record as saying that we don't necessarily need *high* densities to achieve these improvements, we certainly need to do much, much better than sprawl.

But there's a catch: Smart growth lessens the harmful impacts of development not just by concentrating development but also by concentrating impacts. It reduces emissions, runoff, traffic impacts, and intrusions on now-green land regionally in part by increasing them locally. Long-time residents of communities where intensification is occurring sense this intuitively. And that, in a nutshell, is why so many people fear and oppose even environmentally sound development.

All too often, I think smart growth advocates ignore development opposition ("we're right and they're wrong") or simply seek to overpower it politically. (Wise developers, to their credit, often negotiate with opponents, frequently succeeding in getting to a "yes" by making concessions that, in the long run, will save them time and money compared to legal battles. Urbanist policy advocates generally lament these concessions.)

Some pro-development commentators are starting to suggest a different strategy: acknowledge that NIMBY ("not-in-my-backyard") fears are frequently well-founded and address them with changes in design, policy, and process that respect their concerns.

San Francisco neighborhood, 52.5 homes per acre *(image via Bing Maps)*

Boston neighborhood, 52.9 homes per acre *(image via Bing Maps)*

Writing on her planning firm's blog *Placeshakers and Newsmakers*, Susan Henderson suggests that municipal planners trying to win hearts and minds to new development should be more sensitive to building types that fit well with existing neighborhood character. Zoning codes that simply prescribe maximum and/or minimum densities for particular places don't do that, she says, and as a result density targets can be achieved in wildly varying ways that can help or harm a neighborhood.

Consider the contrasting images of a newer neighborhood in San Francisco and an older one in Boston (both aerials and street views are included with this essay). They look and feel totally different. But they achieve almost the exact same neighborhood density, 52.5 and 52.9 homes per acre, respectively. Henderson prefers the Boston example (as do I), but that preference could be for residents to decide. The zoning code should be written accordingly.

San Francisco neighborhood, 52.5 homes per acre *(image via Google Earth)*

Boston neighborhood, 52.9 homes per acre *(image via Google Earth)*

Henderson makes another critical point that both urbanists and environmentalists must grasp: it's the *average* density that matters, not the density of a particular building or parcel. One can achieve a desired density through combining a variety of building types—for example, single-family homes with grassy lots, townhomes, and multistory apartment buildings—working together. There are older neighborhoods in my hometown in North Carolina—and probably in many communities with older neighborhoods—that mix these building types seamlessly, achieving densities much higher than sprawl while retaining a human scale.

It is a tragedy that, at some point, we started outlawing such mixed districts and, instead, began creating suburban pods of identically-sized buildings, places where all the houses are single-family with 1/3-acre lots, or all are townhomes or multifamily. As a result, people interact with others much like themselves, at least in terms of housing preferences, and lack much opportunity to interact with those who aren't. This is the American Dream? We can do better.

My friend Lisa Nisenson is addressing these issues from the process side. When we first met quite some time ago, Lisa was working in what was then known informally as EPA's Smart Growth Office (it had a longer and more bureaucratic name). She has since developed her own business as a consulting community planner. Lisa believes that conflicts over development arise at the "edge" where new development meets old, and that the planning profession has not been sufficiently forward-thinking in respecting the concerns of those who are fearful and creating a framework for resolving them:

> "I've long been frustrated with planning at this edge (having started my planning career in Arlington (VA) as an activist living on this edge but supportive of Metro-oriented density). My main complaints are:
>
> ■ "There are legitimate concerns on livability that can be better addressed if included at the front end of the planning process: noise, circulation, design,

restaurant smells, parks, drainage, parking, garbage pickup, traffic, loading and deliveries, crosswalks.

- "There are also long term impacts that can be better managed when maintenance and management are front-end topics.
- "There is no organized, central repository where local decision makers, developers and homeowners can go to see policies, stipulations, maintenance agreements, photos, plans and graphics that have worked (or fell short) in other places.

"If this is a top reason why good redevelopment and density do not take place [because opposition thwarts it], why are we not addressing it as a planning imperative?"

Lisa has authored a publication titled *Density and the Planning Edge* for the American Planning Association's *Zoning Practice* series. In it, she cites a survey finding that the top three reasons why Americans oppose development are, in order: protecting community character; protecting the environment; and too much traffic. All can and should be addressed early, she writes, through such measures as policies to protect historic resources, design guidelines to protect community character, requirements for adequate park space and tree canopy retention, noise ordinances, and detailed street and transit standards.

But planners may lack familiarity with the right measures. Lisa argues persuasively for a national repository of best practices in preventing and mitigating locally harmful effects of density, and in engaging nearby residents to ensure that their concerns are fairly heard and addressed.

Before closing, I want to make a plug for what I consider one of the best tools for softening density and mitigating the environmental paradox of smart growth: nature. As elaborated in an earlier chapter, I believe that nature has an intrinsic appeal for humans and, if we design density so that it brings more nature into communities, density could become far more appealing and popular.

Quiet green spot amid density, New Orleans *(photo by F. Kaid Benfield)*

And I would particularly urge that the nature we integrate into development—plantings, water, trees, open space, green courtyards and roofs, living walls, and so forth—be designed to serve multiple purposes simultaneously. A menu of choices for multitasking might include, for example, green infrastructure to catch and filter stormwater, places of play for kids and respite for adults, plantings that maximize the absorption of carbon dioxide while releasing oxygen for cleaner and fresher air, green spaces that reduce the heat island effect, and/or signature public spaces to create a sense of place. These can be mixed and matched as circumstances allow, or even all combined into a single space.

It may sound somewhat counterintuitive to link density and nature, but it isn't, really. (Ben Welle, formerly of the Trust for Public Land's Center for City Park Excellence, believes they are mutually dependent.) Even the smallest parcel can make some sort of contribution. As someone in the business of selling more density and urbanity to a frequently distrustful public, I can't tell you how much it would help, and it seriously bugs me that advocacy for urban nature is not a larger part of the smart growth agenda. We'll never make much progress by ignoring the local challenges that smart growth can present.

# More about the Paradox

### How Much Urbanism Is Enough?

Despite the paradox of smart growth, urbanism remains a choice we must make, because the benefits of density can outweigh the detriments, both for the planet and for people. But, as Henderson and Nisenson both suggest, we will do a much better job of it if we identify and mitigate the potential detriments.

For example, what about my spouse, who likes to visit and enjoy cities but likes to retreat from them even more? In her heart she prefers a nature trail or even the relative peace and quiet of a suburban backyard. I've mostly converted her to the smart growth paradigm, and she understands that to save nature we must cluster more in cities. But she's an introvert, and not really a city person by instinct.

We compromised by settling in a relatively quiet, moderate-density city neighborhood, but even there I confess to some irritation when my neighbors (and one aspect of small-lot, city living is that there are a lot of them) seem to think the best way to spend a nice spring weekend day is to bring out some power tools in their back yards and do whatever it is that people with power tools do, loudly. We like to sleep with the windows open, but on nice evenings the 20-somethings in the group house across the street like to hang out on their front porch until the wee hours. Who wants to sleep with earplugs?

Mass transit isn't always the most pleasant and nourishing experience, either (though it sometimes is). So what are we advocating, exactly?

Scott Doyon is one of Susan Henderson's partners in the town planning and development advisory firm PlaceMakers. In his own article on the firm's blog, Scott argues that urbanism has been the right reaction to sprawl but now needs to be tempered to accommodate the human need for occasional retreat from social interaction:

"We...took the suburban promise of independence
and personal space to some pretty ridiculous—and
dysfunctional—extremes but, in attempting to correct them,

we've since made the mistake of confusing the need with the manner in which we satisfied it.

"Simply put, sometimes the last thing we want to do is experience another person. And that's okay. Very few (perhaps none) of us are 'on' all the time. At times, we do need to pull back, to be alone or with intimate gatherings of carefully chosen people.

"Community, for all its benefits, is a tiring endeavor. But that's a hard thing to consider when the larger conversation…is focused on all the measurable ways urbanism can help us solve our problems—from the environmental to the economic to the social."

Scott closes by reminding us that we need to design and build better places for privacy within compact development. Not necessarily more of it, but better. Food for thought.

Walkable but relatively peaceful density, Washington, DC
*(photo by F. Kaid Benfield)*

Wendy Waters, who researches and analyzes urban economic trends and writes the blog *All About Cities*, seems to agree. Comparing locations with different Walk Scores, she suggests that the urbanist Holy Grail of a perfect 100 score may not be for everyone. She likes her own neighborhood (Walk Score 98), but concedes that a high volume of traffic and noise and a lack of privacy can all be aggravating. A still urban but less intense setting might be better:

> "A couple decades ago, few people wanted walkability—they wanted quiet, or the perceived security of auto-centered life. Today, many want the opposite. But maybe we've gone too far in thinking everybody should have everything close by? Perhaps even more people would embrace an urban life with an 85 Walk Score?"

The comments on the post add interesting perspective to the discussion, most of them also using Walk Score while discussing the tradeoffs of urban living. One commenter said that she would gladly give up "ten, twenty, even thirty points" in Walk Score to get away from the noise. Responding to the comments, Waters writes that "in many cities and neighborhoods there are almost-linear balancing opportunities between extreme-walkability-with-noise vs. increasingly quieter or more private living, but a need to walk a few extra blocks."

I think this may be an issue we haven't completely figured out yet. I suppose one too-easy answer is that there never has been and never should be a one-size-fits-all approach to smart growth and urbanism. We can and should provide a variety of environments that offer a range of living choices while staying well within the framework of sustainability. People who value community over quiet should be able to choose that, and vice versa. New urbanism offers the urban-to-rural "transect" as a way of providing different levels of appropriate urban intensity in different parts of a region.

But the availability of choices within urban settings can be tough to realize on the ground, where real-world development occurs in limited-scale, scattered fashion, one parcel here, another there, with developers eager to maximize returns on investment.

In the DC area, I'm not seeing many proposals for moderate density (say, 10 to 20 homes per acre) except in the far outer 'burbs where it won't do much good environmentally, even if builders can find buyers for it. For infill and transit-adjacent projects, I'm seeing plenty of urban intensity, but hardly ever a park or the kind of tranquil, publicly accessible courtyard that can provide an antidote to hyper-urban settings.

Is more attention to moderate density, in more places, part of the answer? Maybe, and so is better design. But perhaps there are other answers, too. That we must have more urbanism is not up for debate, as far as I'm concerned. So let's keep working on getting it right, and making it better.

# 12.

# Design Matters,
# but It Can Be Messy

Contemplating design *(drawing courtesy of Dhiru Thadani)*

This essay was co-authored in 2011 with my friend and frequent writing collaborator, Lee Epstein. (Lee is an attorney and land use planner working for environmental responsibility in the mid-Atlantic region.) As I recall, it was Lee's idea to write about design: Does the architectural character of a building, or streetscape, really matter to a place's sustainability if its performance on emissions and resource use are good? The easy answer would be no. But we think it's more complicated.

As I have discussed in other chapters of this book, many people who live in places undergoing change—and that includes most of us—are fearful of what change may bring. That is true even (some would say especially) if those changes are labeled as "smart growth." This is immensely understandable, particularly given some of the demolition and building that we have witnessed in our neighborhoods over the past few decades. For example, four years ago, Michael Rosen wrote in the New York City neighborhood paper *The Villager*:

> "One by one these [new large buildings] and many other instances pile up and by their height and weight crush the character that makes this place our home. Our diverse ethnicities and income levels, our extraordinary range of interests become mostly homogenized in a relatively rich way. The crucible of our diversity, doubt, dissent and creativity is tied in direct ways to the walkup height of most of our buildings, to affordable rents, to slow streets and the possibility of gathering places and dialogue—neighborhood coffee- and teahouses, local bars, community gardens and their casitas, affordable storefronts and miraculous community centers."

We do not know Rosen's East Village neighborhood or circumstances. But his concerns seem those of a thoughtful resident, not a knee-jerk opponent to all change. The things he believes are threatened by development are the very things that most smart growth and urbanist advocates espouse.

Here's another quote, this one commenting more specifically on building design. Writing in *The New Yorker*, Paul Goldberger described part of an ongoing (and somewhat iconoclastic) revitalization of a faded industrial district in Culver City, California. The project is all about showy, avant-garde design:

> "[Architect Eric Owen] Moss's buildings…may have demonstrated his earnest, if relentless determination to probe different kinds of materials, spaces, and shapes, but I found

it hard to avoid the impression that the main point of a design like The Box—a distorted cube of dark metal on legs that Moss plopped on top of another building—was to make sure that you knew that an architect had been there."

"The Box," Culver City, California *(photo courtesy of Marc Teer)*

Here is yet another, particularly telling passage from the same article:

"The Hayden Tract is as car-dependent as the rest of the city and just as lacking in meaningful outdoor public space in which to enjoy its benign climate. On my last visit, I didn't see anyone walking along the street from building to building, save for a handful of architectural tourists. In one part of the project, five of Moss's buildings face one another across an open space. It's a grand gesture—sharply slanted glass facades and irregular glass canopies define the edges of the space—and a perfect opportunity for a modernist rethinking of a traditional piazza. Instead, it's filled with parking spots."

Again, it's a neighborhood that we don't know personally, and perhaps it will eventually evolve into the arty contemporary quarter that its designers apparently envision. Some of the architecture that appears online is appealing, though the examples published with Goldberger's article are way too in-your-face with iconoclasm to suit most tastes. But, individual buildings aside, right now the district appears to be a long way from a "neighborhood" in any conventional sense of the word. The best one can say is that maybe it's a work in progress that, for the time being, misses an opportunity to create a cohesive community.

It is not debatable that revitalization is critical to sustainability. But it has to be high-quality revitalization, not just a bunch of concrete boxes or high-rises gobbling up a streetscape that was once more invitingly scaled, and not disjointed buildings drawing attention to themselves without relating well to each other and the whole, either. We must be careful what we wish for.

There has been too much mediocrity in the name of smart growth and urbanism, spiced with not a little greed. This is unfortunate, because the character of what we build matters: we who believe that the health of the planet depends on more sustainable development must sell our product, before planning commissions and neighborhood review boards all across the country. If our product isn't more appealing than the alternative—and we don't mean just in the regional or abstract sense but in the local, right-in-this-spot sense—we won't have enough (and maybe don't deserve enough) takers to make our proposition work. We need to advocate the quality of smart growth as avidly as we advocate its quantity.

We have been chipping away at these concepts in our previous writing, in articles with such titles as "Architecture matters," and "Does beauty matter? Should it?"

We think it does, quite possibly a lot. But it sure is messy, because (at least in our opinion) quality and beauty in design don't lend themselves easily to objective measures. We can measure things like transit boardings, impervious surface per capita, vehicle miles traveled, and people accommodated per unit of land. That's what leads us to advocate neighborhood density, transit access, mixed uses, and all the other components of "smart growth" or urbanism, be it of the "new" or old variety.

Oak Terrace Preserve, North Charleston, South Carolina
*(photo courtesy of North Charleston)*

But it's harder to measure what we lose if we can't build enough smart growth to make a difference because what we're offering creates a less appealing place than what was there before.

This is emphatically not, by the way, an attack on "modernism." Some traditionalist friends become apoplectic even at the mention of the word, because they believe so much bad architecture has been built in its name. (There are also plenty of critics on the opposite side, who get agitated by the phrase "new urbanism," in part because of its sometimes-unyielding allegiance to traditional forms. Both groups harbor simplistic views of architectural style.)

For 15 years, NRDC's Washington, DC office was in a very modern, slate-gray building designed by the well-known architects Pei Cobb. It was (and is) an asset to its downtown neighborhood as well as a well-functioning and aesthetically pleasing wokplace. We also love Berlin's modernist Sony Center, designed by Helmut Jahn. Cesar Pelli's design for DC's National Airport is just about perfect, as is the *Gare d'Avignon TGV* by Jean-Marie Duthilleul and Jean-François Blassel. The issue of design quality is not so much a matter of style as one of scale, suitability to context, respect for nature, and perhaps variety.

But isn't design a matter of art and taste, and isn't it presumptuous at the least to impose some kind of artificial standards of taste upon the creative jumble that makes for a great urban experience?

Sony Center, Berlin *(photo by F. Kaid Benfield)*

Would thinking of design as an element of sustainable urbanism, for example, preclude the aluminum, deconstructionist swoops of a Frank Gehry project, or the clean line of a Rem Koolhaas building? Would it prohibit a particular style, or impose some artificial constraint upon the creative process? Would the graceful curve of New York's Guggenheim Museum be limited or, on the opposite side of the spectrum, would the brutalist façade of the FBI headquarters in Washington, DC?

It is not easy, but design is part and parcel of built places, whether we acknowledge it or not. Design can heavily influence the success or failure of the pedestrian experience and, indeed, can even influence how well a place works from a sociological perspective, as in these contrasting examples:

- Increasing personal safety and security with ample windows and porches providing "eyes on the street," or worsening it with long, blank walls;

- Enhancing the shopping experience with easy access, color and movement, or making it less enjoyable with barriers and a drab, uninviting façade;
- Contributing to a feeling of comfort, human interaction, and well-being with green parks and usable, human-scaled open space, or ignoring those characteristics in favor of windswept, characterless plazas;
- Making travel and mobility a pleasant part of the landscape, or forcing pedestrians across multiple lanes of fast-moving traffic or acres of pavement, and making cars the only means of access to office, business, and home.

Gare d'Avignon TGV, Avignon, France *(photo by F. Kaid Benfield)*

Acknowledging the role of design in urban sustainability does not mean micro-managing creativity. It does, however, mean that to truly qualify as smart and green, development cannot simply meet environmental performance goals. It must also be constructed at a pleasing scale, with the materials and building components that welcome people, to get along with its neighbors. New development doesn't have to look just like adjacent development—diversity is good for architecture just as it is good for society and ecology—but it does usually need to be something other than a shocking "sculpture," so unique and artistically precious as to shout: "Look at me. Look how different I am. I am art."

Note the word "usually." There may well be sites and particular uses where the function of having something so utterly different in that place makes perfect sense. Generally, such places and uses are set somewhat apart from the woof and warp of a city's intimate neighborhoods or great streets: the Sydney Opera House, the Baltimore Inner Harbor's National Aquarium, the Milwaukee Art Museum. But these functions and these special places surely can be accommodated in a coherent design philosophy.

In short, design must be addressed in smart people habitat. Not to do so is to ignore how the aesthetic side of the built environment so influences human experience, and how it affects human feeling and function alike. While articulating good design through local regulation may be difficult, that doesn't mean it shouldn't be done—carefully, sensitively, and with an eye toward meeting human needs in the context of place and time.

## More about Design

### Making It Wrong in New Orleans

No big city in America has a local culture—architecture, food, language, music, you name it—stronger and more traditional than that of New Orleans. So why in the world did Brad Pitt's Make It Right Foundation choose iconoclastic architecture in rebuilding homes in the low-income Ninth Ward after Hurricane Katrina?

To an extent the photographs of the project alone tell the story. But here's how my architect friend Victor Dover put it in a Facebook posting:

> "This reflects the sad philosophy that architecture should
> express the violence, chaos, fragmentation and disorder 'of our
> time' (a damaged, damaging phrase, especially after Katrina).
> Instead, we should be establishing order that produces harmony
> and peace in human souls, and creating beauty that drowns

out the threatening aspects of storm and culture, and seeking timelessness—and this will inevitably lead us to designs that are more genuinely resource-efficient and enduring."

Make It Right houses under construction in 2007 *(photo courtesy of Stephen A. Mouzon)*

Good Neighbors? *(Photo courtesy of Stephen A. Mouzon)*

To be fair, whatever one thinks of the architecture, Pitt's houses are all LEED-Platinum, and the fact that he and his charity have taken on the task of rebuilding is a very good thing. But this is a case where design does matter; and these designs look more about the ambitions of the Foundation and its architects than about the community they are serving.

# 13.

# There Must Be a There

Quincy Market, Boston *(photo by F. Kaid Benfield)*

Great cities and great neighborhoods have a distinctiveness about them: when we're in Paris or New York, we know we're in Paris or New York. Within those cities, if we're in the Marais district of Paris or East Harlem in New York, the character and public spaces of those neighborhoods remind us where we are. Unfortunately, there are too many places in America, particularly in newer suburbs, where every place looks more or less like every other place.

In the 1930s, Gertrude Stein famously said of Oakland, California, "there is no 'there' there." Was she saying that Oakland had no anchor, no soul, no *raison d'etre*, no identity? Stein, who was around 60 when she wrote the well-known sentence, had grown up in Oakland, when the city was much smaller. Scholars today insist that she was referring to the loss of places she had known as a child—as in not having a "there" to return to—rather than rendering a general dismissal of the city.

Nonetheless, the phrase has come to refer to places that lack character and distinctiveness. (For the record, I do not find the Oakland of today to be one of them.)

We all know such places, unfortunately. In the new suburbs of America, in particular, every place looks like every other place, or so it seems: wide arterial roads, chain retail and scattered office buildings, subdivisions with near-identical houses, a regional shopping mall here and there that looks like all the others, inside and out. If I drive out of Washington on Virginia Route 123, I quite literally do not know where I am for about ten miles. Am I still leaving McLean? Am I in Vienna? Oakton? I forget—which one comes first? Am I approaching Fairfax? The locations may have different names, but not different identities (until you get to the historic core of Fairfax). The truth is that, because of their equivalence, it doesn't really matter where I am, except as a reference point for my destination.

In a particularly egregious example cited in his classic 1992 book *Edge City*, Joel Garreau described a sizable place in New Jersey everyone simply called "287 and 78" (for the intersection of two Interstate highways). It was a community in the geographic sense, but not in character or in its political administration. According to Garreau, 287 and 78 had no formal boundaries, no elected ruling structure, and no overall leader. Rather, the place was "governed" by a patchwork of generally uncoordinated and conflicting zoning, planning, and county boards. Unfortunately, many places in America can be described much as Garreau described 287 and 78.

Conversely, we all also know places that most certainly do have a "there": when we're in Barcelona or San Francisco, there's little doubt that we are in Barcelona or San Francisco, because the architecture, landmarks, and rhythms of the two great cities tell us so. We also know when we are in downtown Missoula or Asheville; when we're in the relatively small city of Santa Fe, it looks and feels like Santa Fe.

I find that I am almost always thinking about the quality of places. I've had the good fortune to work closely with some amazing architects who have taught me by example how to evaluate places, who have given me a vocabulary to go with my long-held intuitive sense that places feel better when there is, in fact, a "there." The built environment alone cannot give a place character, but it can either help or hurt, depending on whether it supports or diminishes what filmmaker Sarah Marder calls "the genius of a place."

It's not just cities: having a clear identity and distinctive character can be just as beneficial to neighborhoods as to the larger cities that surround them. Often this identity is signaled and enhanced by public spaces. In Washington, for example, a well-known urban neighborhood is called Dupont Circle, because there is an actual place (and wonderful small park) called Dupont Circle that anchors the neighborhood. In Southern California, we know we're in Santa Monica (a city within a city that, to me, feels like a large urban neighborhood) because the Palisades overlooking the Pacific Ocean and beach below remind us, as do the famous pier and pedestrian mall. In London's Bloomsbury or Barcelona's Gracia district, the neighborhoods are dotted with public squares that lend them character.

Why does this matter to greener and healthier cities? Because places that draw us to them are more sustainable, in a quite literal sense. Dupont Circle, like Chicago's Lincoln Park or Kansas City's Country Club Plaza, represents not just a great venue for hanging out but continuity of time, place, and identity. Even in neighborhoods that have faced severe disinvestment, such as Cincinnati's wonderfully named Over-the-Rhine (that story will be in my next book), revitalization is made more feasible because of certain lasting neighborhood anchors, such as Washington Park, the Findlay Market, and the Cincinnati Music Hall. To the extent we use great public spaces to anchor compact people habitat, we reduce the spread of environmental harm.

Placa del Sol, Gracia neighborhood, Barcelona *(photo by F. Kaid Benfield)*

Unfortunately, I think the neighborhood scale is where the environmental movement has had a weak presence over the years. National organizations especially have a feeling, not entirely un-justified, that we can squander our acutely limited resources by focusing on small, individual places. Yet the argument breaks down when one considers that, historically, environmental groups have always been involved in place-based test cases, such as particular wilderness areas threatened by resource exploitation or ecological habitat threatened by highways or oil spills. The truth is that we have never hesitated to focus on places to protect them from harm; why not also focus on places—particularly urban places—as models for what we can do right?

Ethan Kent of the Project for Public Spaces would likely agree. In an eloquent article titled "Placemaking as a New Environmentalism," Kent wrote:

> "It is in fact these immediate environments that humans most directly interact with and experience, and it is this place level or community scale that environmentalism has largely ignored.

We can perhaps best ramp people onto a broader environmental agenda through engaging them in and challenging them to take responsibility for and shape these public realms beyond their homes. This is a process we call Placemaking, which is dedicated to encouraging and empowering people to take ownership over and contribute to the world beyond their private property and work together to improve them. Placemaking is the common sense process through which the human places we most value are created and sustained.

"Only by helping people connect to, care for and shape the world beyond their front doors will we be able to instill people with a capacity to redress the larger environmental crises. Incorporating Placemaking as an essential element of Environmentalism will lead to a reinvention of citizenship and the discovery of new tools and strategies to change the world."

Kent argues that it is not enough to ask whether an action or proposal is doing or likely to do harm: we must also ask whether it is contributing positively to the enhancement of our "environmental, community, social, cultural, historical, and economic" surroundings. Phil Myrick, also of PPS, elaborates in a sort of companion article, "The Power of Place: A New Dimension for Sustainable Development." Myrick writes:

"We feel it is important to give people a proactive approach to sustainability in their hometowns. Creating lively town centers and neighborhoods that enhance pride of place and promote local economic development is critical to improving local quality of life as well as quality of the environment. In fact, we can reinvent entire regions starting from the heart of local communities and building outwards."

I couldn't agree more. When you come down to it, there is no sustainability without places that help limit environmental impacts while also nourishing the human spirit. People habitat—comprising neighborhoods, small towns, cities, metropolitan regions—is every bit as important to the environment as natural habitat and wilderness. Indeed, making human places great should be seen as a key strategy for protecting wilderness. Think about the etymology of the word "attractive": if we attract people to people places, we can better preserve those wild places where we are "visitors but do not remain," to paraphrase the 1964 federal Wilderness Act. But the key to attraction is having a "there" to be attracted *to*.

Mormoiron, France *(photo by F. Kaid Benfield)*

We will not be short of opportunity to make better, more distinctive communities. We will be building homes, workplaces, shops, schools, streets, factories, warehouses, ports, mobility, sources of energy. We need sustenance and we need commerce. To me, the excitement in environmentalism today is found in making our places both sustainable *and* worthy of sustaining. As Kent puts it, "having less impact is noble, but aspiring to have a big impact, to create the world we want starting in the place where we live, work and play, is a transformative agenda." Agreed.

# More about Distinctiveness of Place

## Laissez Les Bons Temps Rouler!

Sometimes the "there" is about more than physical space. In New Orleans, which I mentioned at the end of the previous chapter, it's also about music. No big city in America has a richer local culture or is more steeped in music, without which "New Orleans" would be as hollow an identity as New York without skyscrapers or San Francisco without hills and the Bay. Other US cities host significant amounts of music, of course—the industry hubs in Nashville and Austin, the blues in Chicago; even Seattle, Athens, and Minneapolis had their runs. But in New Orleans, music isn't hosted so much as lived. It's been intrinsic to the city since, well, since there has been a city to speak of.

New Orleans is universally acknowledged as the birthplace of jazz, which begat boogie-woogie, which begat rhythm and blues, which begat rock and roll, which begat funk, which begat hip-hop, and so on. Mix in the French Creole influence and a brass band marching down a street in the Marigny district, leading a "second line" of followers half-walking, half-dancing, strutting to the rhythm, always the rhythm, and heaven help you if you can stay in a bad mood. And, hey, I didn't even get into the Cajun and zydeco parts. Talk to someone from New Orleans and chances are she can tell you the names of ten amazing musicians you've never or barely heard of, and her ten will be better than your ten, no matter how urban-hip you think you are.

It's a city where music is essential to place, and thus to a shared local culture. And, while the big festivals like Mardi Gras and Jazzfest can be fun—more so in the lead-in than the finale, truth be told—it's not really about the biggies. It's about the everyday. You can live in New York for months and not hear or see a Broadway musical. But you can't be in New Orleans for two days without being exposed to the music.

The big events remain significant, though, and not just to the tourist industry. In a sense, they reaffirm the culture, telling the rest of the world, "This is who we are." Carnival music and culture also influence the everyday, as references spring up year-round.

There are lots of Caribbean and Brazilian songs about carnival events. Many of New Orleans' most beloved songs derive from the extravagant—and elaborate—rituals practiced by the famous Mardi Gras Indians. The purple, green, and gold Mardi Gras colors aren't flown just during carnival.

New Orleans *(photo by F. Kaid Benfield)*

If you believe, as I do, that cities are essential to any kind of sustainable future—and if you believe that commerce alone is not enough to make a worthwhile place—then look to the culture. It's why we want to be in a particular place, other things being equal. And it will help a place's sustainability if that culture is both strong and locally grounded.

If a place is going to be cared for, it needs to remind us what is special about it. No major city in the US does that as well as New Orleans—and, if the Crescent City is also about food, language, and attitude, its music comes first.

# 14.

# Human Habitat Should Nourish the Mind, Body, and Spirit

Asheville, North Carolina (*photo by F. Kaid Benfield*)

Although I have spent much of my career analyzing the tangible and measurable, I believe it critical that we not stop there. Indeed, our human habitat should address—or at least be supportive of—the more elusive parts of our overall welfare, providing nourishment to the body, mind, and spirit. Otherwise, what's the point? Surely commerce alone isn't enough. As it turns out, urban thinkers have had a lot to contribute on the subject.

Intriguingly, some urbanists have gone so far as to say that cities can and should be places of healing. The Healing Cities Institute, based in Vancouver, has adopted a "foundation statement" that explicitly connects human health and well-being with physical place:

> "The healing process in the human body is the ability to rebuild, repair and regenerate cells, tissues and organs. Regeneration draws upon the body's innate intelligence to heal itself.

> "What would it then mean for a city to be 'healed,' and eventually to reciprocate and be healing and heal itself, its inhabitants and visitors? Furthermore, what methods and processes would support cities to facilitate healing in the context of sustainability planning? How might the built form and natural spaces of the city nurture and develop its residents' holistic health—to include addressing physical, emotional, mental, social and spiritual needs?"

For those of us who deal in numbers, I'll admit that this sort of language requires a generosity of spirit toward those who have an interest in more elusive concepts. But, the more I think about the true components of sustainability, the more I believe the subjective is every bit as important as the tangible.

The Healing Cities group's statement continues:

> "Key findings in the literature review reveal that healing involves much more than curing physical ailments. Healing is a multidimensional process facilitated by integrating physical, mental, spiritual, emotional, and social components of a person's being. Each component affects the others. This awareness changes the relationship between people and their environments because it recognizes that people do not live as isolated islands, but rather are intimately connected to their surroundings and influenced profoundly by a range of factors."

These concepts do get a bit more specific. Mark Holland, an urban planner and one of the founders of Healing Cities, wrote an excellent essay called "Eight Pillars of a Sustainable Community," in which he articulated the following essential attributes:

1. A complete community (covering land use, density, and site layout; integration of mixed uses and incomes; respect for natural areas)
2. An environmentally friendly and community-oriented transportation system (covering walkability, transit, complete streets, and the like)
3. Green buildings
4. Multi-tasked open space (providing accommodation for both community and environmental needs, with community gardens—"Food should be celebrated in the landscape"—and active and passive recreation opportunities)
5. Green infrastructure (covering stormwater management; water, waste, and solid waste management; energy and emissions; and "eco-industrial networking")
6. A healthy food system (covering food stores, restaurants, farmers' markets, gardens, and festivals)
7. Community facilities and programs
8. Economic development ("encouraging the development of real job opportunities appropriate to the income level of the neighborhood, including live/work opportunities...")

The wording of the Pillars evolved into a very similar but more general set of principles when adopted by the Institute. (Put another way, the Institute employed the language of human aspiration and avoided planning jargon.) For example, "healthy abundance" replaces "economic development"; "restorative architecture" replaces green buildings; "thriving landscapes" replaces open space. If the new language is more ambiguous than the original Pillars, it is also more inviting to non-planners.

Writing in the *Vancouver Sun*, Kim Davis reports that participants in a recent Healing Cities conference "acknowledged the 'woo

woo' stigma that arises among critics at the mention of emotional and spiritual needs." But her article notes also that the city of Vancouver had already begun moving in that direction by explicitly advocating "beauty" in the city's planning policy.

New Orleans *(photo by F. Kaid Benfield)*

Davis spoke with my friend Hank Dittmar, chief executive of The Prince's Foundation for Building Community, who made the case:

> "We thought [talking about zero-carbon housing in a UK project] was a good start, but we thought it maybe ought to be healthy, natural and beautiful as well, so that people would actually want to live in these buildings.

> "It is time to come out of the closet about our spirits."

Holland's Eight Pillars evoke not just the Seven Pillars of Wisdom of T.E. Lawrence and the biblical book of Proverbs, but also the work of another friend, architectural thought leader Steve Mouzon. (I mention Steve's work in a number of these essays.) Steve has articulated a number of essential foundations for sustainable places (nourishable, accessible, serviceable, securable) and buildings (lovable, durable, flexible, frugal).

In a 2011 essay, Steve described "wellness lenses" of body, mind, and spirit through which one can consider the built environment. In each case Steve equates wellness with basic health, or absence of illness, if you will; but he argues that there is also a higher aspiration of "fitness," to which places can also contribute.

Sustainable places can nourish wellness and fitness of body, he writes, with access to healthy food, opportunities for physical activity ("great places to bike, walk, and run"), and reducing the risk of automobile accidents. I would add, and I'm sure that Steve would agree, that clean air and water, and access to a range of health services, are critical components, too. These, too, can be influenced if not entirely controlled by how we conceive the built environment.

Steve believes that wellness and fitness of mind are fostered by the connections that come with true community, and by access to nature. The research certainly supports those points, and I would add that a little peace and quiet helps, too: we need places of reflection as well as of activity and stimulation. While nature—if present—often supplies the former, it does not always do so. I also think that mental health requires urban systems that work well, such as transportation options that relieve stress through comfort, efficiency, and reliability rather than creating it with noise, uncertainty, fear, and congestion. And perhaps above all, our communities and neighborhoods need good schools, without which wellness of mind becomes just about impossible for kids and their families.

Steve reaches some of those points, such as the need for places of reflection, under his discussion of wellness of spirit. He hits his stride in this section:

> "Wellness of spirit increases when we love our neighbors...
> but the co-inhabitants of countless subdivisions aren't really
> neighbors because the places are designed in such a way that
> people seldom meet and speak with each other. So how can
> we love our neighbors if we don't have any?

"Wellness of spirit grows when we do good for others less fortunate. Unfortunately, the American development paradigm has become excruciatingly efficient at separating classes of people in a very fine-grained way so that it is now possible to go interminably through one's daily life in many places in sprawl without ever seeing anyone notably less fortunate. So how are we going to do good for others less fortunate if we never see them?"

Steve continues by stressing the value of time:

"[T]he focus of our built environment in recent decades has been all about getting bigger and getting more. And we've mortgaged ourselves within an inch of our financial lives... or beyond, as many have sadly discovered. Which means that we have to spend countless hours working to pay for it all.

"So it all comes back to time: spending all our time working break-neck for [material] things assures that there's no time left to build our spiritual wellness."

That rings true, if also a bit depressing.

If the quality of our places—our habitat, if you will—can support wellness and fitness, does that mean it can also help us achieve happiness? Don't scoff—it's in our national DNA: the pursuit of happiness is the only basic human right mentioned not just once but twice in Thomas Jefferson's powerfully written introduction to the Declaration of Independence.

Research on the subject finds that good, well-connected urbanism is a significant contributing factor to happiness. In particular, a fascinating study authored by a team from West Virginia University and the University of South Carolina Upstate, and published in 2011 in *Urban Affairs Review*, examined detailed polling data on happiness and city characteristics from international cities. In an article titled "Understanding the Pursuit of Happiness in Ten Major Cities," the authors summarized their conclusions:

Modern man *(drawing courtesy of Dhiru Thadani)*

"We find that the design and conditions of cities are associated with the happiness of residents in 10 urban areas. Cities that provide easy access to convenient public transportation and to cultural and leisure amenities promote happiness. Cities that are affordable and serve as good places to raise children also have happier residents. We suggest that such places foster the types of social connections that can improve happiness and ultimately enhance the attractiveness of living in the city."

(City characteristics are not alone in influencing happiness, of course. The researchers cite a "Big Seven" group of factors recognized by prior study as most substantially affecting adult happiness: wealth and income, especially as perceived in relation to that of others; family relationships; work; community and friends; health; personal freedom; and personal values.)

The researchers drew from an extensive quality of life survey undertaken by Gallup in 2007 for the government of South Korea and published in 2008. Approximately 1,000 people were surveyed from each of ten cities: New York, London, Paris, Stockholm, Toronto, Milan, Berlin, Seoul, Beijing, and Tokyo. Respondents self-reported their overall degree of happiness (measured on a scale of 1 to 5) along with their degree of agreement with a range of statements designed to tease out additional factors.

The team examined the findings, looking for statistically significant correlations. They found confirmation of the Big Seven factors, but also variations that could not be explained by the Big Seven.

In particular, the Gallup study examined a number of questions directly related to the built environment, including the convenience of public transportation, the ease of access to shops, the presence of parks and sports facilities, the ease of access to cultural and entertainment facilities, and the presence of libraries. All were found to correlate significantly with happiness, with convenient public transportation and easy access to cultural and leisure facilities showing the strongest correlation.

The statistical analysis also included questions related to urban environmental quality apart from cities' built form, and produced additional significant correlations:

> "The more respondents felt their city was beautiful
> (aesthetics), felt it was clean (aesthetics and safety), and
> felt safe walking at night (safety), the more likely they were
> to report being happy. Similarly, the more they felt that
> publicly provided water was safe, and their city was a good
> place to rear and care for children, the more likely they were
> to be happy."

Among these, the perception of living in a beautiful city had the strongest correlation with happiness. Curiously, though, the researchers found that the perception of "clean streets, sidewalks, and public spaces" actually had a somewhat negative association with happiness. Happy people apparently find their urban environments both beautiful and messy. (Well, the survey did include New York.)

Arles, France *(photo by F. Kaid Benfield)*

Neighborhoods are particularly significant to connectedness and happiness, the team reports:

> "City neighborhoods are an important environment that can facilitate social connections and connection with place itself...But not all neighborhoods are the same. Some are designed and built to foster or enable connections. Others are built to discourage them (e.g., a gated model) or devolve to become places that are antisocial because of crime or other negative behaviors. Increasingly, researchers and practitioners

have become aware that some neighborhood designs appear better suited for social connectedness than others."

It goes against the grain in today's environmental world to be concerned with things other than tons of carbon dioxide, acres of land, inches of sea level rise, or dollars in a government budget, but for me a concentration only on the objective—or even only on the environmental—can lead to a world (not to mention a vocation) without soul and feeling. I believe we do ourselves and our heirs a disservice if we do not take a more holistic view in crafting our ambitions. If we don't get places right for people, it won't matter what they can do for the environment.

## More about Well-Being

### A Public Index of Happiness

The government of the Himalayan country of Bhutan regularly surveys its citizens on the state of nine key indicators of happiness:

- Psychological well-being
- Physical health
- Time or work-life balance
- Social vitality and connection
- Education
- Arts and culture
- Environment and nature
- Good government
- Material well-being

The use of a "gross national happiness" index has been a policy of Bhutan now for nearly four decades.

Elsewhere, the government of Victoria, British Columbia has participated in a Happiness Index Partnership comprising the Victoria Foundation, United Way, the University of Victoria, and several local and provincial government agencies. The partnership's "well-being" survey has revealed the following:

"Most residents of Greater Victoria experience relatively high levels of well-being. These high levels of well-being are buoyed by strong social relations, feelings of connectedness to community, and relatively low levels of material deprivation for most members of the community. The primary factors that limit a greater sense of well-being across the population are time stresses and the challenges of living a more balanced life.

"There are, however, significant populations who experience lower levels of well-being—particularly low-income earners and single parents. These groups also face substantial time stresses but are less likely to enjoy the material and social supports that help to buttress the effects of the stress on their sense of well-being."

While the overall findings were positive, only 26 percent of the Victoria respondents reported that they spent most or all of their time in a typical week doing things that they enjoyed, according to a summary report. About the same portion reported that "not much" of their time was spent on enjoyable activities. Only 31 percent described their lives as "not very" or "not at all" stressful.

Curiously, some scholars see the study of happiness as a branch of economics, or at least a critical examination of traditional macroeconomics. Among the academic works that discuss it in detail are *Happiness: Lessons from a New Science*, by noted British economist Lord Richard Layard; *Economic Growth and Subjective Well-Being: Reassessing the Easterlin Paradox*, by the University of Pennsylvania's Betsey Stevenson and Justin Wolfers; and *The Pursuit of Happiness: Toward an Economy of Well-Being*, by Carol Graham, at the time a senior fellow in global economy and development at the Brookings Institution.

(The Easterlin Paradox is named for American scholar Richard Easterlin, who found that, within a given country, people with higher incomes were more likely to report being happy. However, in international comparisons, the average reported level of happiness did not vary much with national income per person, at least for countries with income sufficient to meet basic needs. Subsequent researchers, including Stevenson and Wolfers, have found happiness linked to income for both individuals and for countries.)

Proving that even the most upbeat of subjects can be made deadly serious, Brookings has so equated happiness with economics that it chose April 15—"tax day" in the US—to host a forum on the subject in 2010.

# 15.

# Americans Don't Walk Much, and I Don't Blame Them

Crossing the road south of Atlanta *(photo courtesy of Stephen Lee Davis)*

Why don't Americans walk more? Could it be in part because much of what we built between 1960 and 2000 was designed as if walking doesn't exist? The consequences are not pretty.

This won't be breaking news to most readers, but Americans don't walk very much. Periodically, *National Geographic* publishes a 17-nation "Greendex" study on, among many other things, transit use and walking. In 2012 we Americans came in dead last on both indices, and it wasn't close.

In particular, only 34 percent of Americans reported walking to destinations (jobs, shopping, school, and so forth) "often" or "all of the time." Spaniards and Germans walk about twice as much. The rates for Britain and even notoriously cold and dark Sweden were substantially higher than those for the US. Speaking of cold, even the Canadians walk more than we do. We are also dead last in bicycling.

According to census data, the share of workers who commute to work by walking in the US is a measly 6.5 percent; bicycling adds another 1.3 percent. A slim majority of Americans drive alone to work, which also isn't exactly breaking news. (Transit comes in second at 26.5 percent.) Yet research out of Portland State University on "commute well-being" finds that bicycle commuters enjoy their trips to work the most, and those who drive alone enjoy their commute the least.

I suppose there are a number of reasons why we don't walk very much, particularly compared to residents of other countries. But surely a big one is that, for most Americans in most places, walking— that most basic and human method of movement, and the one most important to our health—is all but impossible. Maybe not literally impossible, but inconvenient at best, and tragically dangerous way too often. Except for traditional downtowns, few American communities even have things to walk *to* within safe and easy walking distance.

Walking is downright dangerous along many suburban commercial roads. I suppose it should come as no surprise that sprawling, Sun Belt metro regions built completely around the automobile are statistically the nation's most unsafe places to walk. I reviewed a report released by the nonprofit advocacy coalition Transportation for America in 2011 analyzing traffic fatality data over a ten-year period; the report found that the country's top four "most dangerous" metro regions for pedestrians are all in the state of Florida. Rounding out the top ten are regions in Texas, California, Tennessee, Nevada, and Arizona.

Here are the ten most unsafe metro areas in which to walk, according to the report:

1. Orlando-Kissimmee, FL
2. Tampa-St. Petersburg-Clearwater, FL
3. Jacksonville, FL
4. Miami-Fort Lauderdale-Pompano Beach, FL

5. Riverside-San Bernardino-Ontario, CA
6. Las Vegas-Paradise, NV
7. Memphis, TN-MS-AR
8. Phoenix-Mesa-Scottsdale, AZ
9. Houston-Sugar Land-Baytown, TX
10. Dallas-Fort Worth-Arlington, TX

The organization also reports that more than 47,700 pedestrians were killed in the United States from 2000 through 2009, the equivalent of a jumbo jet full of passengers crashing roughly every month. On top of that, more than 688,000 pedestrians were injured over the decade, a number equivalent to a car or truck striking a pedestrian every 7 minutes.

While pedestrian deaths are usually labeled as accidents by local authorities, Transportation for America believes many are, in fact, attributable to poor roadway design that fails to safely accommodate walkers. Because walking is proven to be good for our health, lowering obesity rates, many people in these unsafe areas are forced to choose between an unhealthy lifestyle or an unsafe one. Children, older adults, and racial and ethnic minorities are disproportionately represented in pedestrian fatalities.

For example, consider Woodbridge, Virginia, about 25 miles south of downtown Washington, DC. A Google Earth satellite image accompanying this chapter shows a section of the area's main drag, the US Route 1 corridor.

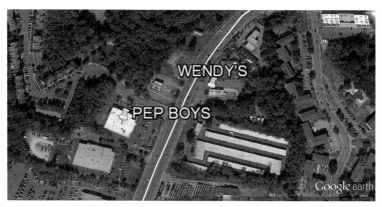

The Route 1 corridor in Woodbridge, Virginia *(photo via Google Earth)*

Home to the Potomac Mills discount mega-mall and not far from the Quantico Marine Corps base, Woodbridge is a diverse "census-designated place and magisterial district" whose population has no majority race but a well-distributed mixture of white, black, Hispanic, and Asian. It consisted mostly of farms and light industrial complexes until the 1980s, when it began attract more suburban development. What you see in the satellite view are, among other things, several auto dealerships and automobile service facilities, some single-family homes, some apartments, a trailer park, and a self-storage facility. All seem sort of plopped down by happenstance.

What you don't see are any but the crudest accommodations for walking. No sidewalks, no crosswalks other than at long-distance intervals; this part of Woodbridge is a place for being either indoors or in a motor vehicle. If you were, say, an employee at the Pep Boys auto parts store on the west side of Route 1, and your spouse had dropped you off and kept the car for the day, and you wanted to grab a sandwich for lunch at Wendy's *right across the street*, you'd have to walk nearly a mile, round-trip, to cross the road with the benefit of a traffic signal. You would lose at least half your lunch hour getting there and back. Even then, half your trip would have no sidewalk.

The view on the road *(photo via Google Earth)*

What many people with limited time would understandably do in that situation, instead, is attempt to cross the road using the shortest and most direct route between Pep Boys and Wendy's, and hope their instincts, quickness, and powers of observation would enable them to do so without getting hit. Some people do exactly that, without consequence.

If a pedestrian does get hit by a motor vehicle, under Virginia law the pedestrian is at fault. In this place, cars come first in the eyes of the law, and anyone who fails to respect that axiom takes chances in more ways than one.

I mention all this because it's more or less what actually happens on this stretch of Route 1. Indeed, in late 2012 two men were hit by motor vehicles while trying to cross the road in separate incidents near the section of Route 1 that I marked. Both pedestrians were evacuated to the hospital, and both were charged by police with "interfering with traffic." The drivers were not charged.

A working single mother in suburban Atlanta named Raquel Nelson wasn't so lucky. In April of 2010, Nelson was charged and convicted of homicide after losing her four-year-old son while trying to cross a busy road after getting off a bus. My friend David Goldberg, who works for Transportation for America, described the facts in a *Washington Post* opinion article:

> "After a long bus trip with her three young children in April 2010, Raquel Nelson did what other bus passengers did that day, and had done so many days before: She attempted to cross the road from the bus stop, which is directly opposite her apartment complex, rather than walk a third of a mile to a traffic light, cross five lanes and walk a third of a mile back, lugging tired children and groceries.

> "The family walked without incident to the three-foot median in the road. As they waited on the median for a break in traffic, Nelson's son A.J. followed other adults who crossed ahead of them. He was hit by a motorist who fled and later admitted to having been drinking and taking painkillers. The driver spent six months in jail and is serving the remainder of his five-year sentence on probation. Nelson

was sentenced last week to 12 months' probation, fines and community service."

Wow. I haven't studied the details of Georgia law or all of the facts, but Nelson's conviction is stunning. Whatever her legal culpability, I find it shocking that Cobb County (northwest of Atlanta) officials chose to exercise their discretion to prosecute her for homicide. David continues:

> "Nelson was found guilty of killing her son by crossing the road in the 'wrong' place. But what about the highway designers, traffic engineers, transit planners and land-use regulators who placed a bus stop across from apartments but made no provision whatsoever for a safe crossing? Those who ignored the fact that pedestrians always take the shortest possible route but somehow expected them to walk six-tenths of a mile out of their way to cross the street? Those who designed this road—which they allowed to be flanked by apartments and houses—for speeds of 50 mph and more? And those who designed the entire landscape to be hostile to people trying to get to work or carrying groceries despite having no access to a car? Are they not culpable?"

(Nelson was granted a retrial and, after further legal proceedings, prosecutors dropped the charge of homicide in 2013. She agreed to pay a $200 fine for jaywalking. According to a news report, the transit agency is considering moving her bus stop closer to a traffic signal and crosswalk.)

For someone who cares about safe and healthy communities, what's the remedy? Jeff Speck's book *Walkable City* provides some answers, but they work best in downtowns and commercial centers. His "ten steps of walkability" to create urban environments that are more conducive to foot travel include such contextually effective measures as placing more housing downtown, restricting free parking, and running transit through dense urban corridors. If we do these things in downtown Boise or Houston or Greensboro or even Bakersfield, it is likely that we will, indeed, make the city more walkable.

Walking to the bus stop in Cobb County, Georgia
*(photo courtesy of Stephen Lee Davis)*

But what the heck can putting a price on parking do for people like Nelson in residential Cobb County or anyone in Woodbridge? Can we have a walkable city where we don't have a city in the first place? What if the location is just a "census-designated place" with a bunch of uncoordinated and unplanned properties that somehow ended up near each other along a high-speed road? The stretch of Route 1 in Woodbridge, in particular, is not remotely ready for more urban measures. The tragedy is that it's urban enough to have some foot traffic, but not urban enough to protect it.

I suppose one answer is that, as the economy allows new businesses and homes to be built in and around the bad stuff, we can gradually make the newer land uses better and more "walk-ready" over time, so that the place can function better for pedestrians when the good stuff reaches critical mass. Meaningful transformation might take a while, though, because many of these places are not the kind of prosperous communities where change can occur rapidly and with the degree of investment necessary to do it right.

Back to Orlando, the region found most dangerous in the country, local officials told *New York Times* reporter Lizette Alvarez that "the data is [sic] somewhat skewed by the number of tourists who visit the state, which inflates traffic." Nevertheless, Alvarez reports that local officials are taking the matter seriously, building sidewalks, installing audible pedestrian signals, increasing traffic calming, modifying bus stops, creating overpasses, and improving lighting.

Whatever the approach, it matters: a lot of places in America are like Cobb County and Woodbridge. And, if we don't start exercising more, including by walking, the prospects for our collective health are daunting. The single most alarming public health trend in the United States today is the dramatic rise in the overweight and obese, bringing serious risks of heart disease, diabetes, and other consequences leading to life impairment and premature death.

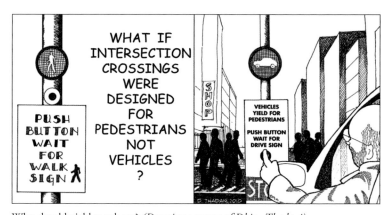

Who should yield to whom? *(Drawing courtesy of Dhiru Thadani)*

While these health challenges are complex, with many factors at play, our country's sedentary lifestyle is an important one. In a massive study of half a million residents of Salt Lake County, researchers at the University of Utah found that an average-sized man weighed 10 pounds less if he lived in a walkable neighborhood—"those that are more densely populated, designed to be more friendly to pedestrians and have a range of destinations for pedestrians"—versus a less walkable one. A woman of average size weighed six pounds less.

Other research has found that men and women age 50–71 who took a brisk walk nearly every day had a 27 percent reduced death rate compared to non-exercisers.

I have some hope for places like Orlando and even suburban Atlanta. As sprawling as they are, there is enough critical mass of residences and businesses to build upon. Bus stops can be much better coordinated with crosswalks at reasonable intervals. But I have a hard time seeing a near-term healthy solution for the Woodbridges of the country.

## More about Walkability

### The Night the 'Burbs Come to Town

My wife and I are lucky to live in a relatively quiet, residential part of Washington, with quite a few things that make it accessible to walkers. Although the houses are not particularly small, for example, they are on modestly sized lots, convenient to each other. Built in the 1920s and 1930s, they are convenient to the street, too: front doors are relatively close to the sidewalks. And, yes, by the way, we have sidewalks, far from a given in the world of today's newer neighborhoods.

The block sizes are small, and we have alleys, too. Streets connect in multiple ways. The intersections have stop signs. The residents, by and large, are a convivial lot. And we have a fair number of kids in the neighborhood.

These things make our part of the city perfect for trick-or-treating on Halloween. It's a big event in our neighborhood.

In Washington, it is easy to tell the city cars from the suburban cars, because they have different license plates. City dwellers have DC tags, while suburbanites usually have tags from Virginia or Maryland. I always expect to see a lot of the latter in our neighborhood on October 31.

Suburbanites come to the city because, in many cases, their neighborhoods are not as walkable. Now, it's not the residents' fault—people choose to live in suburbs for all sorts of understandable reasons. But so many of these developments have been built for privacy, not walking and visiting. Walkways and driveways are longer—in some cases much longer—and may require traversing dark areas. (In our neighborhood, many people park on the street, and those who use off-street garages or spaces access them from the alleys.)

There may be no sidewalks at all. Or, to cite a pattern I have never quite understood, they may have a sidewalk, but only on one side of the street. Lot sizes and block sizes are larger, meaning the kids' distance-to-treat ratio goes way up. Happily, there are exceptions, especially in closer-in suburbs. But it's not the rule.

So on Halloween night suburban parents will drive their kids to neighborhoods like ours and send them around to knock on our doors. (That's exactly what one dad I know has done, driving his kids each year to the nearest walkable neighborhood, about five miles away in his case.) I'm tempted to give the interlopers lumps of coal, but there's no way we're going to take it out on the kids. Maybe some of them will even like the differences, and tell their parents.

# 16.

# Driving Should Be an Option

San Diego *(photo by F. Kaid Benfield)*

Americans' high driving rates contribute mightily to economic waste and environmental degradation. Yet we have built a country in which most people have few alternatives. What can we do in our built environment to turn things around? Fortunately, research provides some clear answers.

I like cars and I like driving. Those who know me well know I'm telling the truth and, if you're looking for a purist manifesto, you've found the wrong book. In fact, maybe it's my 1960s

North Carolina upbringing, but I like *nice* cars and have always managed to have one, thank you very much.

What I would not like, though, is being dependent on a car for every single thing I need or want to do. I also like public transit when it's working well—I've literally met some of my best friends while on public transportation—and I frequently use it for commuting. I *love* walking places, especially city places, and generally manage my daily chores other than commuting on foot. And I'm passionate about bicycling, too, though I ride for fitness, not everyday transportation. I guess you could say that I'm a multi-modal kind of guy, and I feel lucky that my living conditions allow me to practice a life of transportation-by-choice.

I know most Americans aren't so fortunate. Ours is an overwhelmingly auto-oriented landscape, except in a few big city downtowns and older neighborhoods, many populated mostly by residents without kids. Most people have to drive to get to work or school, to go out to eat, to take their laundry and dry cleaning for service, to shop for groceries. If they have children, chances are they are also spending a lot of time shuttling the kids around from one event to another. It's normal, I think, by today's standards. But it's not much fun.

I'm old enough to remember when driving *was* fun. If you can tell a lot about a society's culture from its popular music lyrics, the 1960s were surely the golden age of the American automobile. On July 4, 1964, a new single became the first number one song by that most American of bands, the Beach Boys. Performed with a driving beat and Brian Wilson's soaring harmonies, "I Get Around" celebrated the unequivocal freedom and exuberance that cars provided, particularly on the group's home turf of southern California:

> *We always take my car 'cause it's never been beat*
> *And we've never missed yet with the girls we meet…*
>
> *I get around*
> *Get around, round, round, I get around*
> *From town to town…*

Readers of a certain age may also recall that other hit songs of the 1960s included such paeans to the automobile as "GTO" (Ronny and the Daytonas), "Mustang Sally" (Wilson Pickett), and several more by the Beach Boys, including "Little Deuce Coupe" and "Fun, Fun, Fun." Prince kept up a smidgen of momentum with "Little Red Corvette" as late as 1983.

By the turn of the twenty-first century, though, exuberant car songs were confined to oldies radio stations. If cars show up in lyrics today, chances are that the song is something darker and considerably less innocent than those popular fifty years ago. One can speculate on the reasons, but surely one of the most compelling is that it has been quite a while since driving was "fun, fun, fun" for most Americans.

Instead, driving has become simply a matter of getting from point A to point B, and far too often doing so hampered by traffic congestion and stress, to say nothing of the havoc wreaked on our natural environment. Instead of the open convertibles that symbolized the most desirable cars of the 1960s, sport utility vehicles—essentially complete family rooms (if not fortresses) on wheels that isolate their passengers as much as possible from the external world—became the preferred vehicles of the 1990s and early 2000s.

1969 Pontiac GTO *(photo courtesy of Jack Snell)*

What happened between the golden age of the automobile and today? Just as cars made it possible to expand our communities far beyond traditional downtowns and rail corridors, the act of spreading out—suburban sprawl—placed increasing distances between the various places where Americans live, work, shop, go to school, and worship. The increased distances inevitably led to a tremendous increase in driving: the number of miles driven annually by passenger cars in the US has tripled since the 1960s, reaching a peak of just over three trillion in 2007. While the dramatic growth in driving has begun to slow and even reverse in recent years (in part because of the financial crisis and recession that hit the country beginning in 2008), we still have a long way to go before approaching anything near sustainability.

As a result, traffic congestion has become an everyday menace of American life. According to researchers at Texas A&M University, as of 2011 congestion was draining $121 billion annually from the US economy in the form of 5.5 billion lost hours of productivity—equivalent to 137 million weeks of work or vacation time—and 2.9 billion gallons of wasted gasoline and diesel fuel.

With two-thirds of oil use in the US going to transportation, the average American now uses over twice as much oil as the average person in other industrialized nations, and over five times as much as the average person in the world as a whole. As a result, carbon dioxide emissions from driving in the US remain some 35 percent higher today than they were even as recently as 1990. The US continues to lead the world in per capita carbon emissions, emitting about twice as much of the potent greenhouse gas per person as Germany, the United Kingdom, or Japan, and about three times as much as France.

Given these sobering facts, the challenge in creating sustainable people habitat is to maximize convenience and livability for the community's residents, workers, and visitors while minimizing the burdens on the environment created by the basic need simply to, as the Beach Boys put it, get around. The task is an especially important one, given the relative importance of transportation to energy consumption and corresponding greenhouse gas emissions. A 2007 study reported in *Environmental Building News* demonstrated that the amount of energy used (and greenhouse gases emitted) by a typical office building's operation is dwarfed by the amount that employees and visitors typically consume getting there and back.

To me, the most interesting aspect of Americans' overwhelming dependence on driving is that people's driving habits are not distributed evenly. With the wonderful world of GIS (geographic information systems) mapping, you can see a geographic representation of miles driven per household: those of us in outer suburbs drive a lot more than those of us in more urban locations, whether the latter are in city centers or in the hearts of older towns and suburbs. I discussed this disparity in Chapter 3 in the context of what makes a truly "green" building.

Let's look a little closer at the reasons for the variations. In 2010, transportation uber-researchers Reid Ewing (University of Utah) and Robert Cervero (UC-Berkeley) published a painstaking "meta-analysis" of nearly 50 published studies on the subject of land use and travel behavior. Writing in the *Journal of the American Planning Association*, the two returned to a subject to which they have dedicated most of their careers, in this case updating their previous meta-analysis from 2001.

What they found: When it comes to land use, driving, and the environment, location matters most. The study's key conclusion is that how close a household is to common trip destinations is by far the most important land use factor in determining a household or person's amount of driving. Such "destination accessibility" almost always favors central locations within a region; the closer a house, neighborhood, or office is to downtown, the shorter the average distance one has to drive to other places and the lower one's rate of driving. The authors found that central locations can be almost as significant in reducing driving rates as other significant factors (e.g., neighborhood density, mixed land use, street design) combined.

The clear implication is that, to enable lifestyles with reduced driving, oil consumption, and associated emissions, environmentalists should continue to stress opportunities for revitalization and redevelopment in centrally located neighborhoods. As Ewing and Cervero put it: "Almost any development in a central location is likely to generate less automobile travel than the best-designed, compact, mixed-use development in a remote location."

US Route 29 in Virginia *(photo by F. Kaid Benfield)*

The authors carefully examined each study, applying statistical analysis to tease out which land use characteristics had the biggest impacts on travel behavior when extraneous factors such as income were controlled. After discussing destination accessibility, the authors continue:

> "Equally strongly related to [vehicle miles traveled] is the inverse of the distance to downtown. This variable is a proxy for many [other factors], as living in the city core typically means higher densities in mixed-use settings with good regional accessibility. Next most strongly associated with VMT are the design metrics intersection density and street connectivity. This is surprising, given the emphasis in the qualitative literature on density and diversity, and the relatively limited attention paid to [neighborhood street] design. The weighted average elasticities of these two street network variables are identical. Both short blocks and many interconnections apparently shorten travel distances to about the same extent."

In addition to the effect on rates of driving, Ewing and Cervero also found that, among the characteristics studied, street networks with a high rate of intersections and street connections per square mile are the most strongly correlated with high rates of walking. This makes sense, because a high degree of street connectivity creates alternate routes to destinations, in many cases offering walking distances that are shorter and more direct. Distance to a store was the second most influential factor in influencing walking, with the location and the accessibility of transit next. (Most transit trips begin and end with walking.)

Interestingly, neighborhood density, when separated from the other factors, was found to be less significant than other characteristics in influencing both miles traveled and vehicle trips, although still influential. On its face, this would seem to contradict a substantial body of literature that associates increasing density with reduced driving. Ewing and Cervero suggest that perhaps measures of density are inadvertently acting as proxies for other significant factors ("i.e., dense settings commonly have mixed uses, short blocks, and central locations, all of which shorten trips and encourage walking").

Ewing and Cervero spend a good deal of space attempting to address the issue of "self-selection" or whether, to give an example, people walk more in places with a good walking environment because they are predisposed to walk and choose to live there, rather than because the environment entices them to walk. Reid Ewing explained this to me at some length over the phone a few years back, and I understand it, but I'm not entirely sure it matters. All indications in the market suggest that we have a large, growing, unmet demand for close-in, walkable neighborhoods and an emerging surplus of automobile-dependent environments.

Unless that unmet demand for close-in, walkable environments somehow turns into a surplus, which isn't happening anytime soon, building more of them will reduce driving and increase walking. The environment doesn't care about psychological motive. In any event, the authors found in this case that applying research controls for self-selection might, if anything, show an even more significant influence of land use on behavior.

The best news is that Ewing and Cervero have found that the effects of the various individual factors studied—location, transit, connectivity, land use mix, and design—are additive in reducing driving and increasing walking. If a municipality or developer is able to take advantage of (or strengthen) all of them, the result will be a more sustainable development than if some are missing. What Ewing and Cervero (and all the researchers whose studies they analyzed) have given us is a science to go with the art of better placemaking.

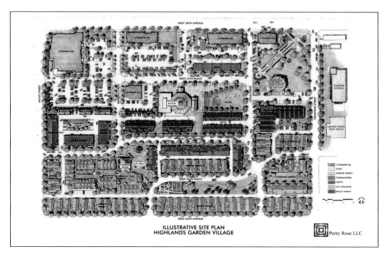

This Denver development has well-connected streets
*(rendering courtesy of Perry Rose)*

So, what about people such as myself, who enjoy driving sometimes when it's a matter of choice? Can we as a society get back to the optimistic, exuberant feelings of driving in the early 1960s? Maybe not: we have done some damage to the planet since then, and these are more sobering times for other reasons, too. If we can reclaim exuberance, it is unlikely to be because of cars and driving. But we can start down the road, so to speak, and being more thoughtful about our built environment can help.

Our goal should be to create more driving-optional neighborhoods. Achieving it will be harder to accomplish in suburbs and smaller towns than in cities, but even in less accessible locations we can still plan and design our communities more thoughtfully to encourage walking and shorter driving distances, and make a difference. Given the massive increases in population expected for the US and elsewhere over the next half-century, we had better.

# More about Reducing Driving

### Going Car-Free in Vauban

I've never been to Vauban, an experimental inner suburb of Freiburg, Germany, near the Swiss border. But I've seen lots of appealing photos of it and read about it, including in a particularly engaging 2009 article by Elisabeth Rosenthal in *The New York Times*.

Rosenthal writes that street parking, driveways, and home garages are generally forbidden in Vauban, whose streets are completely car-free with few exceptions. Those include the main thoroughfare, where the tram to downtown Freiburg runs, and a few streets on one edge of the community. Car ownership is allowed, but owners must park at the edge of the development, where one can buy a space for $40,000.

As a result, 70 percent of Vauban's families do not own cars, and 57 percent sold a car to move there. "When I had a car I was always tense. I'm much happier this way," Heidrun Walter, a media trainer and mother of two, told Rosenthal.

Standard vehicles in Vauban *(photo courtesy of Eigen Arbeit)*

Completed in 2006 and home to 5,500 residents within a rectangular square mile, Vauban may be the most advanced experiment in low-car suburban life in the world. The community has "its own unusual gestalt in the country that is home to Mercedes-Benz and the autobahn," to use Rosenthal's phrase. It apparently helps that Vauban's shape is long and relatively narrow, so that the tram into Freiburg is an easy walk from every home. It also has mixed uses, with stores, restaurants, banks, and schools more interspersed among homes than they are in a typical suburb.

Most residents use bicycles to get around and have carts they haul behind their bikes for shopping trips or children's play dates. (It must not be hilly.) There is a car-sharing service along the likes of ZipCar in the US (or Car2Go, a company that started in Germany and that is now making headway in the US market), which residents use for trips to larger stores or to the ski slopes.

Moreover, the community's commitment to sustainability goes beyond transportation. All of Vauban's homes are built to be hyper-energy-efficient, and some buildings are heated by a district heat and power station burning wood chips, while others have solar panels. The community's 59-home "solar settlement" is said to be the first housing community in the world in which all the homes produce a positive energy balance. The solar energy surplus is then sold back into the city's grid for a profit on every home.

Vauban was built on the site of a former French military base, and is named after Sébastien Le Prestre de Vauban, a 17th century Marshal who built fortifications in Freiburg while the region was under French rule. Construction began in the mid-1990s.

# 17.

# Getting to School Shouldn't Be So Hard

Walk to School Day *(photo courtesy of US Department of Transportation)*

When I give talks about the issues in this book, I frequently ask my audience, "How many of you walked or rode a bike to school as a kid?" Hands go up all over the room. Just about everyone aged 40 or older. Then I ask, how many have kids who walk to school now? A few hands go up, generally well under ten percent of the room, even though half or more may have children.

As recently as 1973, some 60 percent of school-age children walked or biked to school. I'm told that, today, the portion is about 13 percent. All this while we have a serious problem with childhood obesity, which has more than doubled in children and tripled in adolescents in the past 30 years, according to the National Centers for Disease Control. What's wrong with this picture?

Saratoga Springs, in upstate New York, is a relatively affluent small city popular with tourists and known for its historic architecture: the Saratoga Race Course, which has been hosting horse racing since 1863, and Saratoga Spring Water, which has been bottled in the community since 1872. There are mineral springs all over town. Its Performing Arts Center is the summer home of the Philadelphia Orchestra and the New York City Ballet.

In other words, Saratoga Springs is the kind of old-fashioned place where one might hope to find kids walking or biking to school. Not so, it turns out. A 2009 story initially reported by Andrew J. Bernstein in *The Saratogian* attracted attention from urbanists all over the country when the Maple Avenue Middle School enforced a policy against riding a bike to school, even on national Bike to Work Day. The fact that the student was riding alongside his mom didn't seem to matter, according to Bernstein's article:

> "Janette Kaddo Marino and her son, Adam, 12, wanted to participate in the commuting event, so the two set off to Maple Avenue Middle School on bicycles May 15. The two pedaled the 7 miles from their east side home, riding along a path that extends north from North Broadway straight onto school property.

> "After they arrived, mother and son were approached first by school security and then school administrators, who informed Marino that students are not permitted to ride their bikes to school."

Ironically, the Saratoga Springs School Board had declined to apply for a state grant to improve things under the state's Safe Routes to School program. In this case, of course, safety concerns were minimized by the fact that the kid was riding on a dedicated trail separated from traffic and with adult supervision. Adam and Janette Marino were also experienced cyclists, having ridden as a family from Buffalo to Albany along the Erie Canal.

Biking not encouraged in Saratoga Springs *(photo via Google Earth)*

The policy is certainly over the top, taking power to judge kids' safety out of their parents' hands, but I can't say that it is irrational. The problem is the school's location, completely isolated from its community instead of placed within the community where walking and bicycling would be a much more convenient and common choice.

Perhaps the policy has been relaxed by now. Bernstein wrote in a comment on my blog that the school board had agreed at least to consider it, and also that the Marinos continued to ride together to school with the school board's assent.

A little over a year later, I ran across a similar story from Laguna Beach, California. It was another special event: national Walk to School Day (or, as some places called it, "Walk and Roll to School Day"). In 2012 over 4,000 schools around the country participated in the event, including 495 in California, from Eureka to Atherton to Beverly Hills to Long Beach.

But Laguna Beach said nope, not here, according to a 2010 article by Cindy Frazier in the *Laguna Beach Coastline Pilot.* Not even for one day did the city want its kids getting to school via any mode other than a motor vehicle. It's just not safe, they argued, probably not without some reason, given California traffic. But riding in a car isn't exactly safe, either, given that each year some 250,000 children are injured in automobile accidents, including the 2,000 kids who die as a result. Motor vehicle accidents are the leading cause of death for children between ages two and 14.

As it turns out, there isn't much within walking distance of Laguna Beach's public schools, anyway. Of the four schools in the Laguna Beach Unified School District, only the high school is centrally located; Thurston Middle School and the two elementary schools are all on the fringes of the developed area.

Frazier writes:

"Unfortunately, the school district is right: It's just not safe or practicable in Laguna Beach for most kids to walk or roll to school.

"But [complete streets advocate Les] Miklosy is also right: In some neighborhoods, kids could walk or bike to school. But that's not a lot of kids."

Here is the particularly disheartening part:

"Demographics, politics, and economics have incrementally eliminated the neighborhood school…[School district representative Norma] Shelton reiterates these issues in a response to an e-mail from the *Coastline Pilot*:

"Our district is committed to teaching 'lifelong fitness' and has robust physical education and athletic programs. However, in Laguna there are few sidewalks, winding roads with blind corners and a considerable distance for our students to travel and we cannot endorse walking or biking to school so much so that, at considerable cost (parents pay a portion), we provide busing for the elementary schools and middle school."

Is this any way to build a child-friendly community?

Thurston Middle School, Laguna Beach *(photo via Google Earth)*

Accompanying this chapter is a street-view photo of Thurston Middle School. Notice how the sidewalk actually stops at the school entrance, guaranteeing that any kid who dares to walk to school will find herself immediately in the path of motor vehicles. And that definitely would not be a good thing: parental traffic at Thurston, chauffering kids to and fro, has apparently gotten so heavy and unwieldy that the school published a flyer full of sternly worded cautionary rules and a complicated-looking traffic flow map.

The Thurston dads have formed a volunteer "strike team" of on-site traffic managers whose motto is "get in, get it done, get out!" Parent or kid, sounds like a nice way to start your day, no?

Frazier observes that another school in Thurston's district, El Morro Elementary, is basically near nothing, not even the community of Laguna Beach itself. It does sit on the Pacific Coast Highway, across from the surf, and no doubt has a spectacular view; it could hardly be closer to what in theory should be a terrific amenity for the kids. But it's hard to imagine that they get to enjoy it much, given the traffic in between the school and the beach.

As of the 2010 census, there were 10,281 households in Laguna Beach, 20 percent with children under 18. The median annual income for a family is $156,115, two and a half times that of the US as a whole. The median value of an owner-occupied home there is "$1,000,000+" according to census data.

Kids from forty countries participated in Walk to School Day, which continues as an annual event. In the US, walking and cycling to school may no longer be the norm, sadly, but at least for one day thousands of parents, kids, and communities make an exception. Michelle Obama has promoted the event. Typically, there are volunteer escorts, special treats, and the like, to make sure that it is safe and fun. As a result, a lot of kids love the event, and it helps people see what might be possible if a little more attention and more thought were paid school design and location. In Washington where I live, it is celebrated on every local TV station. Even former federal Transportation Secretary Ray LaHood participated when he was in office.

But, in Laguna Beach, it's just another day in the O.C.

# More about Schools and Community

### Principles for "Smart Growth Schools"

Schools used to be the heart of a neighborhood. Children and not a few teachers could walk to class, or to the playground or ball field on the weekend. Walking was relatively easy, because the schools were placed within, not separated from, their neighborhoods. Their scale was welcoming and their architecture was not just utilitarian, but signaled their importance in the community.

I'm not the only one who would like to see a resurgence in neighborhood-based schools. For those of us who are interested, there is a website dedicated to providing resources on "smart growth schools." The site, which includes a well-annotated "report card," a listserv, links to some very good resources, and a pathway to hands-on assistance, was created by Nathan Norris, who has been developing community performance indicators for at least a decade.

The report card, which is designed to assess community policy toward schools, is especially good, with 24 pages of great tips and advice based around eleven key principles:

1. *Restoration Preference:* Will old schools be restored rather than replaced so long as the cost is less than a new school? This is a separate question than whether the school building will be recycled for another use (i.e., adaptive reuse).

John Eaton Elementary, Washington *(photo by F. Kaid Benfield)*

2. *Holistic Planning:* Is school planning done in conjunction with land planning and transportation planning or are these segregated?

3. *Community Buy-in:* Is the school planning process designed to secure meaningful community input prior to decision-making?

4. *Elimination of design constraints:* Does the community have the flexibility to size and design the school efficiently to fit into the site and the neighborhood?

5. *Neighborhood School:* Is the school embedded into a walkable neighborhood so that most students can reach it safely without traveling by car or bus?

6. *Prominent Site:* Is the school sited in a prominent location (e.g., terminated vista or on top of a hill) so that it communicates the importance the school has in the culture of the community?

7. *Shared Use:* Is the school sited or designed so that it can share uses with the community such as a gym (or YMCA), park, ballfields, community meeting space, day care,

library, performance theater, art studio, cafeteria/restaurant, community garden, or health clinic?

8. *Flexibility:* Is the school designed so that it can grow (independent additional wings, floors, or structures) or contract in size and services (areas can be removed or adaptively reused if no longer used for school purposes) as the neighborhood grows or contracts so that it remains useful over a longer period of time?

9. *Connected Learning Environment:* Does the school connect itself to effective distance learning opportunities; is the school connected to the local community through interaction with local businesses or through a community service program?

10. *Community Pride in the Design:* Is the school designed so that it generates community pride as measured by a Visual Preference Survey (VPS)?

11. *Green building certification:* Does the construction or renovation of the school follow best practices regarding energy efficiency, water efficiency, indoor air quality, daylighting, light pollution, and earth-friendly construction techniques as set out in the LEED for Schools program?

That's a heck of a list. Well done.

# 18.

# Walk, Drink, Walk Back

Homestead bar, San Francisco *(photo courtesy of Craig Howell)*

If we can take the measure of a person by the company he or she keeps, perhaps we can take the measure of a neighborhood by whether there are good "third places" to keep company. I wouldn't go so far as to say that a good bar is all it takes to make a neighborhood great, but it's a relevant indicator. And there are many good reasons for that bar to be in walking distance of its clientele.

My friend Eliot Allen first introduced me to the concept of neighborhood completeness: that the quality of a place is defined in part by how many different basic functions it has in close proximity to homes and to each other. Eliot was closely involved in the creation of the LEED for Neighborhood Development green rating system, and the concept made it into the system. LEED-ND gives credit toward certification for a development that contains, or locates near, certain categories of "diverse uses": supermarket, pharmacy, restaurant, child care facility, library, and so on.

I was part of the LEED-ND team as well, and I note that we did not list "bar" or "pub" as a creditworthy neighborhood asset. But Michael Hickey, a community development consultant, makes a good case for their inclusion as "third spaces," or community hangouts. In an article titled "In Praise of (Loud, Stinky) Bars" and posted in the National Housing Institute's *Rooflines* blog, Hickey writes:

> "The vaunted 'third space' isn't home, and isn't work—it's more like the living room of society at large. It's a place where you are neither family nor co-worker, and yet where the values, interests, gossip, complaints and inspirations of these two other spheres intersect. It's a place at least one step removed from the structures of work and home, more random, and yet familiar enough to breed a sense of identity and connection. It's a place of both possibility and comfort, where the unexpected and the mundane transcend and mingle.
>
> "And nine times out of ten, it's a bar."

I have never seen a better description of why good drinking establishments can hold such appeal, can even play a significant role in knitting together this elusive concept we call "community."

Author Ray Oldenburg first coined the phrase "third places" in his 1991 book, *The Great, Good Place*. His arguments for creating and sustaining such neighborhood places were good ones then and, in these current times of electronic communication and chain retail, may be even more compelling today.

Later in the *Rooflines* article, Hickey posits that bars support community life in a valuable way that other establishments do not:

"We shouldn't romanticize third spaces as only being about brightly lit cafes, pedestrianized streets, and the local public library. Bars work in their scruffy way by offering a place to get away from an overcrowded apartment or a squalid loft or a grimy job. They are a place where someone with little to spare can go for a change of pace…

"The goal of a bar patron is to enjoy the primary benefit of any decent third space: a place to linger. I'm still looking for someone to generate a 'lingering index' so that we can measure the impact of just plain old hanging out—but that's really at the heart of place-making, and we shouldn't forget it."

I love the idea of a "lingering index."

What does this have to do with sustainability? Well, quite a bit, in my opinion. The more complete our neighborhoods, the less we have to travel to seek out goods, services, and amenities. The less we have to travel, the more we can reduce pollution from transportation. People enjoy hanging out in bars and, especially if they are within walking distance of homes, we can also reduce the very serious risks of drinking and driving.

On that subject, Scott Doyon of the planning and development advisory firm PlaceMakers has gone so far as to map "pub sheds," or five-minute walking zones from pubs in the Atlanta suburb of Decatur. Writing in his firm's excellent blog *PlaceShakers and NewsMakers*, Scott concludes that his community is fairly well covered. He further suggests that, if one extends the walkability zones to ten-minute distances, it would be well-covered indeed.

Like Hickey, Scott salutes the contributions that neighborhood bars can make to community cohesion:

"My town of Decatur, Georgia—already pretty walkable, especially by Sun Belt standards—has, for the past 15 years or so, been developing a thriving pub scene. In addition to some long-time institutions already in place, we now have a growing number of neighborhood-friendly taverns spread around town.

A pub in Decatur *(photo courtesy of Chloe Fan/chloester)*

"These are where neighbors go, hang out, and get to know each other, and they've contributed to the fact that, here in Decatur, craft beer has pretty much become a de facto component of the city's economic development strategy."

Later in the article, Scott adds that, "If ever there was a business you should be walking to (and from) rather than driving, it's your bar." Agreed.

I lived in Decatur for a bit when I was completing my under-grad studies at Atlanta's Emory University, a few minutes away by car in those days. My girlfriend was a student at Agnes Scott College, a pretty campus in the heart of Decatur. There were some classic bars a few miles away from Agnes Scott that fit Hickey's description of a "scruffy" place where we could go to hang out. But they were in Atlanta, not Decatur, and not within walking distance of where either of us lived. It's good indeed to see the fine concepts of drinking, lingering, and walking merge in my old territory.

I might add that, in the download age—which has already killed all but specialty music stores, weakened movie theaters, put print newspapers on life support, and finished off all but a few bookstores—the remaining places where there is a sort of shared community commons are becoming ever more important. Bars qualify: you can't download a pint of Guinness.

## More about Reasons to Walk

### How Far Are We Willing to Walk Somewhere?

There are a number of good informal tests to determine a community's walkability. In the blog I write for NRDC, I've described the popsicle test (can a child comfortably walk to buy a popsicle and walk back home?), the Halloween test (does the neighborhood attract kids walking door-to-door on Halloween?), and the 20-minute neighborhood test (can you meet most of your daily needs within a 20-minute walk or transit ride?). My friend Steve Mouzon, whose common-sense thinking about our built environment makes several appearances in this book, adds the tourist test (is a place good enough that people will want to vacation there?); Scott Doyon, as described above, likes the "pub shed" (how many drinking establishments are within walking distance?).

In evaluating reasonable walking distance, LEED-ND adopted the conventional wisdom that transit-inclined people will walk as far as a quarter-mile to a bus stop or a half-mile to a rail station. For those who like comparative numbers, the increasingly sophisticated online service Walk Score calculates the number and types of typical destinations within comfortable walking distance of any given location and assigns a rating based on the outcome.

But Steve has now added another, very interesting idea to the mix: he posits that, in fact, "comfortable walking distance" is not a constant but a variable, and that the distances we are willing to travel on foot depend on the quality of the environment along the way. Steve calls his concept "Walk Appeal." Streets and neighborhoods that entice us to walk farther have greater Walk Appeal.

This street in Santa Monica has high Walk Appeal *(photo by F. Kaid Benfield)*

In Steve's provocative blog *Original Green*, he illustrates the idea by comparing two different environments that produce very different outcomes. First, he describes a chain retail shopping experience:

"Walk Appeal…explains several things that were heretofore either contradictory or mysterious. It begins with the assertion that the quarter-mile radius (or 5-minute walk), which has been held up for a century as the distance Americans will walk before driving, is actually a myth.

"As we all know, if you're at Best Buy and need to pick something up at [a nearby] Old Navy, there's no way you're walking from one store to another. Instead, you get in your car and drive as close as possible to the Old Navy front door. You'll even wait for a parking space to open up instead of driving to an open space just a few spaces away…not because you're lazy, but because it's such a terrible walking experience."

For a captivating city such as Rome, however, Steve notes that people happily walk much, much farther "and then keep on walking without ever thinking of driving."

Continuing, Steve suggests that one will walk two miles or farther in a world-class city such as London or Paris, but "put a Parisian accustomed to walking five miles or more per day on a suburban American cul-de-sac, and they wouldn't walk much." He further posits that people will walk about three-quarters of a mile on a good American Main Street, where building entrances tend to be along the sidewalk, with narrow storefronts to provide variety in the walker's view. For residential areas, Steve says that, if a neighborhood is or mimics a traditional (pre-1950) one, we typically will walk about a quarter of a mile. But in sprawling suburbs, the distance drops to about 250 feet, and in a power center of big-box stores the distance drops to 100 feet.

In his post, he elaborates:

> "People won't walk across a sea of parking to get to another store because the walking experience is simply too dreadful. This is exacerbated by the fact that a sea of parking is a heat island, capturing and storing the sun's heat in all that dark asphalt, raising the temperature of the air above it by dozens of degrees in summertime. A sea of parking is also a huge stormwater runoff problem, and is most often solved by building really ugly stormwater retention pits nearby. If you don't know what they are, a retention pit is a depression several feet deep in the ground, usually surrounded by an ugly chain-link fence, where all the styrofoam cups, packing peanuts, and plastic wrapping collects after a rain."

So, one could say that a street in the heart of a world-class city has much more Walk Appeal than a typical suburban American street, and that a traditional Main Street has more Walk Appeal than big-box stores separated by a large parking lot. That, in a nutshell, is the concept of Walk Appeal.

This parking lot in Hillsboro, Oregon, not so much.
*(photo courtesy of CMH-90/Chris)*

Intuitively, I think Steve is on to something here. His theory is supported by a body of thought about the characteristics that make an appealing walking environment—sidewalks, traffic safety, shade trees, visual variety, and so forth. But there are all sorts of variables and additional factors to consider:

- **Purpose.** To an extent, I think Steve's examples compare apples, oranges, pears, and grapes. We travel in different places for different reasons, which affect our willingness to walk. In particular, to make Steve's American-retail-versus-Rome comparison a fair one, a hypothetical traveler would have to be on the same sort of journey in both scenarios. Best Buy is an electronics store. Shoppers purchasing, say, televisions are unlikely to walk two miles to another shopping destination, even if they have the option of walking down Rome's finest street to get there.
- **Personal safety.** A long walk that is visually appealing but in a sketchy area is unlikely to have much Walk Appeal,

even if its urbanism suggests that it should. Also, does Walk Appeal vary by time of day? I suspect it does; I'll walk farther in daylight than in the dark, unless it's oppressively hot in the daytime.

- **Convenience and time.** I will indeed walk two miles in parts of New York or Paris or Washington if I can spare the time, but depending on terrain, climate, crosswalk interruptions, and other factors it will probably take me somewhere between 30 and 45 minutes. If I'm in a rush, I'll take a cab.
- **Nature.** I will walk farther if I can traverse or at least walk alongside an appropriately sized (not too big) and well-designed park on the way to my destination. In fact, I will deliberately lengthen my journey in order to go through a great park such as the Jardin du Luxembourg in Paris, mentioned in an earlier chapter.
- **Alternatives.** Just as there are places where walking is a terrible experience, there are places where driving is a terrible experience. Heck, there are places where public transportation is a terrible experience, too. We weigh the costs and benefits of our choices and may walk farther if the other options are poor.
- **Environmental intensity.** In one of Steve's blog posts, a commenter suggested that "people density," creating a sense of liveliness, is helpful. I would agree, but to a point. Crowds can be oppressive and can slow one's walk. Sound matters, too: music can be helpful, but construction noise is a killer for walking.

So, is Walk Appeal more art than science? It feels a little in-between to me. We can describe some of its elements, but not all of them are easy to measure.

What I like best about the concept is the suggestion that a comfortable or pleasant walking distance is highly variable, and that part of the reason we choose to drive even short distances is that sometimes the experience of walking to them is so horrible. Steve has provided some useful new vocabulary and an interesting frame through which we can evaluate streets and neighborhoods.

I'm all in on those ideas, and think Steve came upon a "Eureka!" moment when he found a way to articulate it. But my hunch is that, for me at least, it is the idea of Walk Appeal that has power, and I would caution against a quantitative or definitive application.

# 19.

# Successful Suburbs Will Adapt to the Twenty-First Century

New vision for Dublin, Ohio *(rendering by Goody Clancy, courtesy of city of Dublin)*

The Columbus, Ohio suburb of Dublin was immensely successful in the 1980s and 1990s, attracting prominent corporations and affluent residents. It was built in a completely automobile-dependent, spread-out manner, however, and that doesn't trend well for the twenty-first century talent Dublin's corporations must attract to remain competitive. The city is doing something about it.

By almost any conventional measure, Dublin, Ohio is a wildly successful community. For starters, it is one of the wealthiest municipalities in Ohio, with a median family income of $126,402 (as of 2010), more than double that for the nation as a whole. Unlike older Midwestern cities founded on an industrial economy, Dublin is a modern community that has experienced tremendous growth in recent decades, with fewer than 4,000 residents as recently as 1980, but upwards of 38,000 today.

Dublin is now home to the headquarters of Wendy's, Ashland, Cardinal Health, and several other corporations, including the new-technology company OCLC (originally Online Computer Library Center). Nationwide Insurance and Verizon have significant presence there. The Professional Golf Association's Memorial Tournament, one of the PGA's most prominent events, is hosted annually by Ohio native Jack Nicklaus. The Scioto River runs through the heart of town, which also boasts a very pleasant historic district.

It's all working. So, one may wonder, why change anything? The answer is that Dublin's leaders are thinking like a business. They know that their success has been based on a late-twentieth-century suburban form that is now becoming outdated: office parks, malls, single-family subdivisions, and a near-total reliance on the automobile. Having been on the leading edge of past suburban success, they want to be on the leading edge for the twenty-first century as well. And right now, although they have great assets to build upon, they suspect that they aren't ready for the new generation of "customers."

Outside of the relatively small historic district, for example, Dublin's main transportation corridors are lined with development that is relentlessly automobile-oriented, unwalkable, and frequently bland. While visitors may see an affluent community, they will also see a disjointed one that resembles nothing so much as run-of-the-mill sprawl, so typical of suburbs built in the 1980s and 1990s.

As recent city manager Terry Foegler told Holly Zachariah of *The Columbus Dispatch* in 2009, Dublin has been missing what it needs to attract young professionals and empty-nesters: "a trendy, urban area in which to work, play and live."

Some residents have rightly voiced concern that historic character be preserved as change occurs, but Eric Leslie of the Historic Dublin Business Association echoes the need to evolve. Leslie told Zachariah that development that would get people to live downtown, ease walking and biking in the area, and give residents something to do would be wonderful: "We need an area where people can stroll and hang out, where people can have some fun. What we need is an energy."

Dublin, Ohio in 2009 *(photo courtesy of Dougtone)*

In response, the city council commissioned the Bridge Street Corridor Study, a bureaucratic name for an evaluation and planning exercise to determine whether parts of the community's central area could be re-imagined to accommodate more walkable, livelier development. Technical support was provided by Goody, Clancy & Associates, an architecture and planning firm that has advised clients all over the country—and the world, for that matter—on contextually appropriate urbanist makeovers. Bridge Street is Dublin's principal east-west artery (though it takes other names along the way); it runs through the heart of commercial Dublin and the historic district.

The planning culminated in late 2009 and 2010, and both the process and the findings were well received. Goody Clancy began the right way, listening to businesses and residents, while also bringing in nationally recognized experts including Chris Leinberger, Laurie Volk, and Carol Coletta to offer perspective on development trends and markets. All advised that the community should go walkable and mixed-use to position itself for the future.

"Honestly, I don't know that any part of it came as a complete surprise to me, particularly in terms of housing stock and the kind of lifestyle environment that young professionals might be seeking," council member Tim Lecklider told Jennifer Noblit of *ThisWeek Dublin* in late 2009. "I've been saying for several years on council that we probably have a full complement of single-family homes for a community of our size. To build any more could create a glut of that type of housing."

Noblit's article indicated that other council members were in general agreement, though some had an understandable concern that the makeover occur in the right places. Council member Richard Gerber told Noblit that evolving to accommodate twenty-first-century lifestyle preferences could be seen as "the natural progression of things. We built a town and now we have fine neighborhoods that have attracted business. I think in some way this is just one more part of the process."

From talking to residents, businesses, and community leaders, Goody Clancy found that Dublin is facing increased competition from downtown Columbus, other suburbs, and other parts of the country for the young talent needed to supply the diverse, skilled workforce sought by modern employers. "As many as 60,000 people work in Dublin in the course of a year," Foegler told Philip Langdon of *New Urban News* (now *Better! Cities & Towns*); between 5,000 and 8,000 employees are hired every year in the community.

Goody Clancy subcontractor and market analyst Zimmerman, Volk Associates found that, while "there [was] projected demand for about 1,500 housing units over the next 5-7 years in the study area," most of that will be for housing more suited to singles and empty nesters than the community's current housing stock. Indeed, as further evidence of a changing attitude, the high-tech OCLC is already pursuing walkable development alternatives for the 80 acres it owns in Dublin.

Goody Clancy's inquiry recognized that it is important to build in a way that strengthens neighborhoods, not just adds to them; that development should enhance, not diminish, the town's historic district and character; that transportation choices and more complete streets would be required; and that the community's greenway and open space network should grow.

The firm found that the Bridge Street Corridor offered a particularly significant redevelopment opportunity because it contained several large parcels of land under single ownership (including commercial properties well past their prime), and several property owners seeking higher-value uses for their land. Focusing on the corridor also presented opportunities for increasing connectivity and transportation access, while avoiding impacts on the community's single-family neighborhoods, which mostly lie outside the study area.

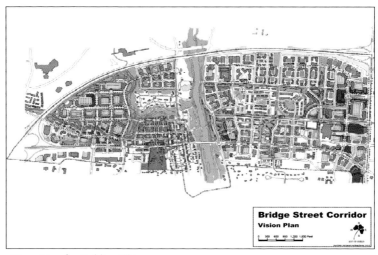

New vision for Dublin, Ohio
(*rendering by Goody Clancy, courtesy of city of Dublin*)

Goody Clancy focused on neighborhoods, key arteries with potential for improvement, and expanding the park and trail system. Differentiating the recommendations by sub-districts and neighborhoods, they illustrated how the city could achieve a future with these outcomes:

- The Bridge Street Corridor is Dublin's centerpiece. Dublin's historical and cultural heart is strengthened and balanced

by highly walkable districts and neighborhoods on both
sides of the Scioto River.

■ Exceptional green spaces preserve the outstanding natural
features in the corridor and seamlessly connect each unique
district along the corridor.

■ Mixed-use districts bring together complementary
arrangements of living, working, and recreation in
memorable settings created by distinctive, human-scaled
architecture and streets that invite walking and gathering.

■ Greatly expanded choices in housing, employment,
activities, and transportation attract new generations of
residents, businesses, and visitors.

■ The Bridge Street Corridor radiates a diversity and vitality
that mark it as a special place not only within Dublin, but
within the region, nation, and world.

The plan, now being implemented, is ambitious, integrating
new development amidst a fair amount of retained existing buildings. New facilities include townhome, multi-family, and loft housing; new office space; new shopping and civic facilities; roof gardens;
a trail network; and even space for a light rail line.

Reinforcing Goody Clancy's insights about Dublin, urbanist trend-spotter Richard Florida has written in *The Wall Street
Journal* that, to do well in today's economy, suburbs need a bit of
urban character:

"Just a couple of decades ago, the suburbs were the very
image of the American Dream, with their sprawling, large-lot
homes and expansive lawns. Suburban malls, industrial parks
and office campuses accounted for a growing percentage of
the nation's economic output. Planners talked about 'edge
cities'—satellite centers where people could live, work and
shop without ever having to set foot in major cities.

"With millions of American homes now 'underwater' or in
foreclosure, the suburbs and exurbs have taken some of the

most visible hits from the great recession…The suburbs that have continued to prosper during the downturn share many attributes with the best urban neighborhoods: walkability, vibrant street life, density and diversity. The clustering of people and firms is a basic engine of modern economic life. When interesting people encounter each other, they spark new ideas and accelerate the formation of new enterprises. Renewing the suburbs will require retrofitting them for these new ways of living and working."

Later in his article, Florida reiterates that suburbs that take steps to become more walkable and urbane will be well-positioned to compete for the creative class (a phrase he coined):

"Walkable suburbs are some of America's best places to live, and they provide their sprawling, spread-out siblings with a model for renewal. Relatively dense commercial districts, with shops, restaurants and movie theaters, as well as a wide variety of housing types, have always been a feature of the older suburbs that grew up along the streetcar lines of big metro areas…

"These are the places where Americans are clamoring to live and where housing prices have held up even in the face of one of the greatest real-estate collapses in modern memory. More than that, as my colleague Charlotta Mellander and I found when we looked into the statistics, the U.S. metro areas with walkable suburbs have greater economic output and higher incomes, more highly educated people, and more high-tech industries, to say nothing of higher levels of happiness."

In 2012, the Dublin City Council unanimously adopted an overhaul of its development and zoning code to accommodate the Bridge Street vision and purchased land to accommodate some of the changes. When the vision is fully realized over the coming years, the city expects the district to accommodate 8,000 new homes (most of them rentals in multi-family buildings) and over five million square feet of new office and retail space. Yet Dublin also expects to double the amount of city-owned open space in the corridor from 60 to 119 acres. Rather than relying on past success, Dublin is once again seizing the moment to adapt and grow.

## More about Remaking Suburbs

### A Green Showcase to Replace Failing Big-Boxes

June Williamson, co-author of *Retrofitting Suburbia*, and landscape architect Anne Vaterlaus have designed a very appealing illustrative design for an aging site in the LA suburb of Pico Rivera, on the edge of the San Gabriel Valley. The community is working-class, 92 percent Latino, and relatively low-income. Air pollution levels are high.

Their proposal is conceptual, not real, at least not yet. But if the site, now a big-box "power center" with a Walmart, a Lowe's, a Staples, and so on, isn't ripe for a new concept yet—and I'm not saying that it isn't—it's just a matter of time. (The Walmart, incidentally, was the site of a major labor strike against the retailer in 2012.) Here's how Williamson described the site and the designers' concept on the blog of the BMW Guggenheim Lab:

> "Pico Rivera Towne Center was a subsidized 'magic bullet' project that was cynically (or naively) conceived to fill municipal coffers with sales tax income while providing mostly low-wage jobs. It is now—predictably, perhaps—failing.

> "We considered how this site might be retrofitted once again, with more resiliency, by introducing a retooled model based on production, designed around training, employing, housing, and feeding a local labor force in need of skills and opportunities. We propose replacing surface parking with transit-served inclusionary infill housing and a day labor station. We propose reusing big-box stores for vocational

schools and training programs. We envision reinhabiting the massive warehouse buildings with green, clean energy R&D and local food-processing facilities serviced by spurs to the existing freight rail corridor. We also encourage growing food—vertically, hydroponically, and in terraces—within and around the warehouses, as well as expanding self-provisioning through community gardening at the river's edge."

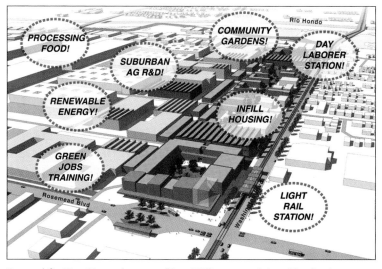

Proposal for Pico Rivera *(courtesy of June Williamson and Anne Vaterlaus)*

As discussed in an earlier chapter, the existing Pico Rivera development is hardly the first "Towne Center" that in fact is neither town nor center. America's suburbs are full of similar "grayfields" and grayfields-to-be: malls and big-box stores surrounded by surface parking lots, built for a limited lifespan, and becoming abandoned or significantly downgraded as their initial uses run their course. These places harm the environment and their communities, especially when the first generation of stores moves on.

Grayfields pose both a huge problem and a huge opportunity, as sites become available for recycling into better, greener uses. Kudos to Williamson and Vaterlaus for pointing the way.

# 20.

# Childhood Should Be about Exploring

Boy exploring creek *(photo courtesy of Tom Woodward)*

My wife Sharon and I often marvel at how highly scheduled and supervised the lives of our friends' kids seem to be. Although we grew up in different circumstances, Sharon in a ranch house in a then-new suburb of DC and me in an apartment close to the downtown of a small North Carolina city, we both have fond memories of wandering, exploring, and following childhood whims in our neighborhoods. I could be wrong, but exploration seems rarer these days.

Instead, we have activities by appointment, almost all of which require car trips out of the immediate neighborhood and parental accompaniment. Say the phrase "soccer mom" and everyone knows what you mean: a mom who taxis her kids around to scheduled activities from the time they can walk, many of which do indeed involve soccer and most of which involve continued supervision. Some years ago a study by the Surface Transportation Policy Project found that a typical suburban mom spends the equivalent of 17 full days per year driving, more time than the average parent spends bathing or feeding a child.

There's nothing wrong with soccer dates—soccer is "the beautiful game" and I'm a fan—but when do kids and their friends get to decide for themselves what to do and, within some reason, when and where? When do they get to learn that grownups also lead their own, independent lives? I have some very happy memories of tossing baseballs, basketballs, and especially footballs with my father; and I played the usual kids' team sports. But, if my parents had been there for every practice and every game, as seems to be today's norm, I would have gone absolutely batty. I would have been embarrassed.

I won't pretend to understand all the reasons why parents today seem more reluctant to encourage their kids to explore on their own—surely they are complex—but here are a couple of ideas:

- Parents are afraid, especially of abduction or harm from strangers (though statistically these are no more common today than when I was a kid).
- Our culture of spread-out living and car dependence means fewer sidewalks, more car trips, more dangerous automobile traffic, perhaps weaker friend networks in neighborhoods, and less free time.

All this is implicit in a wonderfully written and provocative essay by Michael Chabon, published in *The New York Review of Books* in 2009. It is so good that I am tempted to reprint the whole of "Manhood for Amateurs: the Wilderness of Childhood," but instead I'll give you a taste:

"When you went out into those woods behind our house, you could feel all that history, those battles and dramas and romances, those stories. You could work it into your games, your imaginings, your lonely flights from the turmoil or torpor of your life at home. My friends and I spent hours there, braves, crusaders, commandos, blues and grays.

"But the Wilderness of Childhood, as any kid could attest who grew up, like my father, on the streets of Flatbush in the Forties, had nothing to do with trees or nature. I could lose myself on vacant lots and playgrounds, in the alleyway behind the Wawa, in the neighbors' yards, on the sidewalks. Anywhere, in short, I could reach on my bicycle, a 1970 Schwinn Typhoon, Coke-can red with a banana seat, a sissy bar, and ape-hanger handlebars…

Boy in Jardin du Luxembourg *(photo courtesy of Tom Ricker)*

"Childhood is, or has been, or ought to be, the great original adventure, a tale of privation, courage, constant vigilance, danger, and sometimes calamity. For the most part the young adventurer sets forth equipped only with the fragmentary map—marked here and there by tigers and mean kids with air rifles—that he or she has been able to construct out of a patchwork of personal misfortune, bedtime reading, and the accumulated local lore of the neighborhood children."

That's the way it should be, Chabon argues, but not the way it is:

"I have been to Chicago maybe a half-dozen times in my life, on book tours, and yet I still don't know my North Shore from my North Side, because every time I've visited, I have been picked up and driven around, and taken to see the sights by someone far more versed than I in the city's wonders and hazards. State Street, Halsted Street, the Loop—to me it's all a vast jumbled lot of stage sets and backdrops passing by the window of a car.

"This is the kind of door-to-door, all-encompassing escort service that we adults have contrived to provide for our children. We schedule their encounters for them, driving them to and from one another's houses so they never get a chance to discover the unexplored lands between. If they are lucky, we send them out to play in the backyard, where they can be safely fenced in and even, in extreme cases, monitored with security cameras. When my family and I moved onto our street in Berkeley, the family next door included a nine-year-old girl; in the house two doors down the other way, there was a nine-year-old boy, her exact contemporary and, like her, a lifelong resident of the street. They had never met."

I want to go on and on, but you should read it for yourself. Two great bloggers found Chabon's essay before I did, and made some thoughtful observations relevant to community planning. First, John Michlig, writing in his blog *Sprawled Out: The Search for Com-*

*munity in the American Suburb*, echoes Chabon's thoughts and relates them to his own community of Franklin, Wisconsin:

"Another sad victim of suburban non-planning is the ability of our children to enjoy the freedom of wandering a 'territory' of their own. Our children now need to be escorted via car to pretty much every event in their lives. Even the occasional decently sidewalked subdivision is enclosed by wall-of-China collector roads that are impassible and limit safe travel.

"A few nights ago the local news featured the story of a child hit by a car in a nearby suburb. A neighbor pointed out the road it happened on; a typically winding, wide, pedal-to-the-metal subdivision speedway. The kid made the mistake of riding his bike a few hundred yards from his house in the hostile environment we currently embrace.

"There was talk of an ice cream shop going into Andy's on Rawson and 51st (still planned, as far as I know). Sadly, it's a horrible idea—who would let their child travel there independently, crossing 51st or Rawson? Yet, there it will likely stand, beckoning for—- cars. We will drive our children there, and they will have their ice cream under our sheltering eyes."

Second, Sarah Goodyear, writing in *Streetsblog*, echoed that what is most stifling to kids' freedom today is a preponderance of streets that are unsafe because of automobiles. Indeed, the Robert Woods Johnson Foundation has cited data indicating that kids who live near heavy traffic will have a five percent increase in Body Mass Index, on average, compared to those who don't. The implication is that they are less likely to expend their energy walking outdoors, because it is perceived as unsafe.

In an earlier post Goodyear makes the point that, while parents fear to let their kids ride public transit independently (the city bus was a godsend when I was a kid) or walk a few blocks, they think nothing of driving them everywhere. But car crashes, she reports, are the leading cause of death for kids in the US.

Just in time *(photo courtesy of pawpaw67/Ed L)*

Now, the odds of dying in any one car trip are certainly low. But Goodyear goes on to quote Lenore Skenozy, the author of the provocative book *Free-Range Kids*. Skenozy says that, compared to the dangers of automobile travel, "the chances are 40 times slimmer that your kid walking to school, whether or not she's the only one, is going to be hurt by a stranger." And she would learn independence, an important life skill to acquire before one enters adulthood.

As I write this, I will soon be visiting my own mother, now in her ninety-third year. She's in a different sort of wilderness now, a sad one, but I am so glad that she and my father had a few other things to do when I was growing up and allowed me to find my independence. Would I have become a tennis player if I hadn't been able to find my way on foot to the courts a mile from home? Would I have become an environmentalist if I hadn't explored the woods on my own? Would things have turned out differently if every activity had required a car trip? Those were the days.

# More about Inter-Generational Community

## The Elusive Goal of Aging in Place

Most aging adults want to remain in their own neighborhoods as their housing needs change and their comfort level with driving wanes. But few of our newer communities provide a variety of housing options so that a senior citizen could, perhaps, downsize from a single-family home to an apartment without leaving the neighborhood. Fewer still provide good transit service or shops and amenities within a safe and easy walking distance—critical for seniors who can no longer drive. For example, my mother's home was at the end of a long driveway in a neighborhood without sidewalks. When it became difficult and eventually unsafe for her to drive, she found herself more and more isolated. This is all too common among seniors.

Safe crossings are critical for seniors
*(photo courtesy of www.pedbikeimages.org/Dan Burden)*

Fredrick Kunkle summarized the unfortunate consequences in an article published in the *Washington Post*:

- Older nondrivers are likely to make 15 percent fewer trips to the doctor, 59 percent fewer trips to stores or restaurants, and 65 percent fewer trips to social, family, or religious gatherings.

- 3.6 million nondrivers older than 65 stay at home on any given day.
- Six hundred thousand people aged 70 and older stop driving every year.
- More than 20 percent of Americans 56 and older do not drive.
- The number of senior citizens is expected to double by 2030.

Some charities and informal groups are heroically pitching in to drive folks around. They deserve medals. But guess what: finding volunteers to do the driving is difficult because most of the people who are available during the day are retired and themselves elderly. Kunkle cited one case in which an 80-year-old drove a 60-year-old cancer patient to the doctor's office; the scheduled driver for the follow-up trip was 87.

One of the answers to this problem—and maybe the most important one related to the built environment—is to build communities that contain a variety of housing types and prices, including facilities for seniors. Another is to build neighborhoods that are safe, convenient, and interesting for all, including nondrivers and people with special needs. Transit service is critical if people are to reach destinations beyond walking distance. But, for most cities and towns, these are long-term solutions.

What to do in the meantime? I wish I had better answers.

# 21.

# Grow Food,
# but Not Just Anywhere

A community garden in Boston *(photo by F. Kaid Benfield)*

Community gardens and urban farms have become immensely popular. This is a very good thing, so long as they support rather than displace important city functions. Growing spaces should fit into the urban landscape, not turn city neighborhoods into the country.

I am somewhat amazed—and definitely pleased—by the extent to which access to healthy local food has become a city planning concern in a relatively short time. Very few planners and urbanists were talking about this issue before 2005 or so. Now the movement includes everything from initiatives to address food deserts (neighbor-hoods without places to buy fresh food) to urban farming to agricultur-al suburbs. On the food desert issue, I'm a strong believer in incentives to open neighborhood stores selling produce, or walkable supermarkets, to provide convenient access to fresh food to as many people as possible.

The extent to which I support community gardens and urban farms, however, depends on the context. I think we still need cities to be cities—walkable, compact places of urbanity—and we still need the countryside to be the countryside in order for both to reach their full potential for sustainability. Indeed, the two are mutually depen-dent: we need cities and suburbs with compact footprints in order to preserve farmland and other natural resources outside of the devel-oped area. I support growing food within urban or suburban devel-opment *if* the garden or urban farm does not compromise walkability and a nonsprawling regional development pattern.

For example, I'm a huge fan of so-called "victory gardens," a phrase that originated during the World Wars of the twentieth cen-tury to describe family-sized plots for growing food in cities and sub-urbs. Frequently grouped together on parkland near urban apart-ments where residents do not themselves own land, victory gardens are leased to individuals or groups to be tended. The gardens were intended to help America deal with food shortages during wartime, when much of the country's industrial and agricultural effort was be-ing directed to support the military; there was also a shortage of farm workers because so many of them were serving their country abroad. This was back when people on the home front actually had to pitch in to sacrifice and assist a war effort. Imagine.

We have them tucked away all over Washington, including some within walking distance of my house. They are immensely popular. *Wikipedia* reports that victory gardens produced up to 40 percent of all the vegetable produce consumed nationally during World War Two. Government campaigns emphasized to home front urbanites and suburbanites that the produce from their gardens would help lower the price of vegetables needed to feed the troops, thus saving money that could be spent elsewhere on the military: "Our food is fighting," one poster read.

Poster from World War I
*(photo courtesy of US Department of Agriculture)*

Another great example of the kind of city garden that I love is the one on the rooftop of the DC food charity Bread for the City, with 30 beds for growing vegetables. The nonprofit green roof organization DC Greenworks assisted with the set-up, and Bread for the City's clients are helping with the tending. In an article written on the local blog *DCentric*, Elahe Izade described some of the benefits of the rooftop garden:

"[T]his garden won't be able to feed all Bread for the City clients (the organization serves 4,500 families a month — that's a lot of food for a roof to produce). Instead, it will primarily serve as a way to educate clients and the community about food justice and also serve as a green space 'to foster reflection' and spur dialogue between and among clients, community organizers and donors about food sustainability."

That's good stuff.

The country is now dotted with community-tended gardens in almost every city, and that's a good thing, too. One of my favorites in this genre is the Pisgah View Community Peace Garden, in a public housing project in my home town of Asheville, North Carolina. The Peace Garden is the brainchild of resident Robert White and his wife, Lucia Daugherty, who saw a vacant, trashed-out patch of land on the property as an opportunity "to work with the kids, engage parents and stress the importance of reciprocity," meaning that neighbors help each other, and those who contribute are rewarded by enjoying the results of their and their neighbors' labors.

The garden contracts with local families in a CSA, or community-supported agriculture, agreement that supplies subscribers with fresh, local produce. Senior and disabled Pisgah View residents share the bounty free of charge, according to a story by Aiyanna Sezak-Blatt in the local weekly *Mountain Xpress*, and people are welcome to trade work in the garden for food. The Peace Garden also hosts classes on sustainability and local community events.

With the tag line "your partners in grime," the Peace Garden's website summarizes its mission:

"Pisgah View Community Peace Garden (PVCPG)…is continuing to grow as an organization that will seek to provide fresh local organic food to the community. In addition, the organization will strive to make this food available to elderly, disabled and homeless populations through its social programs. Furthermore, PVCPG has established educational programs to help schools, churches and youth groups learn about the importance of local sustainable agriculture. Finally, the garden is always building partnerships with a diversity of organizations and businesses looking to create a healthier Asheville community and healthier planet!"

I am old enough to remember when the Pisgah View public housing complex was built many years ago, on a hillside now overlooking a freeway interchange, a heavily used bridge, and a neglected urban river far below. This is not the sort of walkable, beautifully designed, mixed-income, mixed-use project that I usually write about: this is old-style public housing, not unpleasant in its way but of another era. It has few sidewalks, minimal landscaping, marginal upkeep, and not much within safe walking distance. The project has a lot of mileage on it, so to speak, and the Peace Garden has now injected it with a strengthened sense of community and pride, as well as with a source of healthy food.

Rooftop garden, Bread for the City, Washington, DC *(photo by F. Kaid Benfield)*

To support urban density and walkability, urban agriculture means the right kind of farming (e.g., vegetables, not sheep), at the right scale (small), and in the right spots (where other, more traditionally urban, uses are not displaced). In a pedestrian-oriented retail district near a transit station, for example, urban density and smaller, people-oriented open spaces (whether green or hardscape) make more sense than crop or fruit cultivation, as a well-meaning organization proposed for a highly urban Chicago site in 2010. Fortunately, that proposal was eventually withdrawn.

Similarly, I am skeptical of larger farms of up to 40 acres or more in cities, as I have heard proposed from time to time. Particularly in cities whose suburbs are continuing to expand, big urban farms can perversely take city land that might otherwise be developed, forcing new development out onto real farmland. In an email to me on the issue, Jane Kirchner of the American Farmland Trust was particularly articulate:

> "Farmland is somewhat like habitat in that big landscapes are important and fragmentation tends to degrade the resource value. When farmland is surrounded mostly by other farmland, it tends also to be close to abundant equipment, supplies and services. When farmland is surrounded by urbanization, these resources are harder to find and more costly to access.

> "Where agriculture should be woven into the urban fabric is where it can help support high quality density. Community gardens, edible (as opposed to purely ornamental) landscaping and farm plots on school grounds, for instance, can all add value to urban neighborhoods. These practices are still too rare and should be encouraged. Setting aside whole fields within development principally for food and fiber production where those fields are not also providing open-space services needed to support density is a mistake."

I don't want to say that there will never be a situation where a large tract for growing food could be responsibly accommodated in a city. But I certainly believe it should remain an exception, not the rule.

And then there is the matter of the agricultural suburb, where developers use onsite farming as an amenity to lure potential residents farther outside the city. Dressing up an outlying subdivision—perhaps once a real farm—with a farming theme just creates a kind of sprawl-in-disguise not unlike the faux "net-zero" housing development I profiled in this book's second essay. For example, a development called Serenbe, promoted by its website as "under 30 minutes from Atlanta's Hartsfield-Jackson International Airport" (apparently assuming no Atlanta traffic; sure), currently has about 170 residents and a 25-acre organic farm on a whopping 1,000-acre site.

The heart of Serenbe *(photo via Google Earth)*

Serenbe is basically being promoted as a commuter suburb and I predict it will become one, just a very high-end one with open space and a farm as amenities for residents to enjoy. The development is sometimes touted as "new urbanism," but there is nothing urban about it. When its privately owned open space is accounted for, it is actually much more sprawling than conventional sprawl.

In another example, a 538-acre development in British Columbia *way* outside of Vancouver was proposed in 2009 as "agricultural urbanism," promising up to two thousand homes, along with "50-acre farms and perhaps one 160-acre farm." The idea—and I really wish I were making this up—was to justify encroachment on real farmland by saving remnants of the former farms for the new residents to enjoy. I don't think that one was ever built. In reality, the "agricultural urbanism" would have been neither agricultural nor urban.

We are losing an acre of farmland every minute to development, according to the American Farmland Trust.

What we need is a compact regional development footprint, with conserved farmland *outside* that footprint. Daniel Hernandez, planning director for the Jonathan Rose Companies, says it best:

> "Finally, after so many decades, policies for smart
> agricultural policy are just now emerging into some level of
> coherence, and building support. It is clear that agricultural
> land preservation is critical to the economic future of
> our country and to feeding our country. Anything that
> undermines that would be irresponsible.

True farmland in Pennsylvania *(photo courtesy of Merry Rabb)*

> "Recognizing that much of this prime land around
> the country has unfortunately already been infringed
> upon, there is every reason to still support the complete
> preservation of these spaces. Our challenge as planners,
> developers and policy-makers of the built environment in
> an era of climate change is to figure out how to strengthen
> agriculture systems and biodiversity of our farmlands, and
> connect them to livable cities and their consumers. Our
> intention should be to support policies that preserve these
> valuable resources and strengthen their economic viability,
> not to assist in their destruction."

Food gardens and smaller urban farms in the city? Absolutely. With perhaps rare exceptions, larger farms belong in the true countryside.

## More about Farming in the City

### The Grow Dat Youth Farm

In a city that is perhaps the country's most culturally rich, it is a bit surprising that the large city park in the heart of New Orleans is called, well, City Park. But don't be fooled by the generic name— City Park is home to the much more colorfully named Grow Dat Youth Farm, which is developing a sense of responsibility, community, environmental stewardship, and service among local high school kids through the collaborative work of growing food.

Grow Dat grew out of a partnership developed between the Tulane University City Center, the New Orleans Food and Farm Network, and City Park. Its program is sophisticated. From Grow Dat's website:

"The farm works with several high schools and youth organizations throughout New Orleans to recruit a diverse and committed group of youth who develop leadership and life skills during their intensive, hands-on work experience. Through a structured application process, Grow Dat conscientiously recruits a mix of students: 20% of whom have already demonstrated leadership skills inside or outside of school, 20% of whom are at-risk of poor performance at school, and 60% of whom are students that are neither excelling nor failing at school. Programmatic success is defined by students' consistent participation in the program, their increased ability to communicate effectively with other students and staff, and their ability to achieve production goals on the farm…

"Over the 19-week program, youth participants learn a variety of skills related to growing, cooking and selling organic vegetables and fruit. Full time Grow Dat staff have created a curriculum that includes lessons on sustainable agriculture, cooking, communication and team- building, economics, nutrition and community health, food systems, and the agricultural history of our region."

The Grow Dat kids sell their wares *(photo courtesy of Grow Dat Youth Farm)*

The students must commit to a work schedule, for which they are paid. In addition to the work they perform on site, they are expected to take their experience to the larger community:

"Working in rotating teams, students take on the responsibility for selling food at farmers' markets and preparing food for homeless or underserved populations. In addition to these hands-on activities, students also participate in a highly-structured system for enhancing their communication skills called 'Real Talk'... In addition to improved communication skills, students are also trained on time management, effective strategies for team work, and public speaking—all skills that can be broadly applied in future jobs."

The farm enjoys a central location accessible by public transportation. It is located on a four-acre site in City Park, with two acres of cultivable land.

With the assistance of the Tulane School of Architecture, buildings on the Youth Farm's site have been designed to serve the program. The campus includes green building innovations for the facilities, including an outdoor classroom, a teaching kitchen, locker rooms, administrative offices, and large post-harvest handling areas.

One of Grow Dat's quarterly reports notes the friendly competition between students at a local farmers' market to see which crew could sell out first. The report also notes that every kid had the opportunity to prepare and serve their produce at a free monthly breakfast hosted at a local church. Over three months they served over three hundred meals, learning "important, and sometimes surprising, lessons about what the face of hunger in our community looks like." The students' goals for 2013 include growing 9,000 pounds of food, donating 40 percent to needy families, and selling the rest at farmers' markets.

# 22.

# Cities Are Made for Faith, and Vice Versa

Calvary Baptist Church, Washington, DC *(photo courtesy of Elvert Xavier Barnes Photography)*

I grew up as a Bible-Belt Methodist, and my immersion in that culture had a profound and lasting effect in shaping my values. While I no longer adhere to a particular faith, I remain intensely interested in and comfortable with discussions of church teachings, particularly those related to ethics. This drew me to the work of a number of city-based religious practitioners and thinkers, whose views I profile in this essay. Although these theologians are Christian, I believe their urban values apply much more broadly.

I have an elusive relationship with religion. That's probably not very unusual, given the inherent unknowability of it all. But I suspect those of us who carry around an uncertainty regarding things spiritual may experience it in very distinct ways.

I was raised as a Protestant Christian in western North Carolina, right in that part of the southeastern US where evangelical Protestantism thrives and church attendance is high. I went to revivals as a kid; there's a Billy Graham Freeway in my hometown. Probably nine-tenths of my social life revolved around the Methodist church, one way or another. While I no longer observe religion in the same way as then—at this point, I would probably be some mixture of Unitarian Universalist and Buddhist if I practiced at all, which I don't, generally—my religious upbringing had *everything* to do with my values of peace, justice, and stewardship.

I am who I am today because of who I was then.

It strikes me as odd that strongly-held religious beliefs have become associated with conservative politics in the US. For me, spiritual values remain essentially liberal ones: ethical practice means understanding and caring for others and showing decency and respect, not condescension. I know: easy to say, not always easy to do.

As a result, when I run across people of faith who are also environmental and urbanist leaders, I pay special attention. They are, in a sense, speaking in a language that is deeply embedded in my consciousness. When I hear of impressive faith-based initiatives for urban revitalization, such as those by Bethel New Life in Chicago, I'm rooting for them a bit harder than I might otherwise.

Along these lines, I was especially glad to run across an excellent essay on religion and the city some time back by Aaron Renn, author of the *Urbanophile* blog. Renn writes:

> "Urbanists should take religion much more seriously than they often do. That's because it plays a much bigger role in the city and civic health than currently believed, and because many urban congregations have mastered the art of outreach and conversion in a way that transit and density advocates can only dream about.

"Churches have always been important institutions in cities. Even today, the only reason many families with children are confident enough to stay in the city is because they can enroll their kids in Catholic or other religious schools. I can only imagine what a place like Chicago would look like if its religious school network wasn't there. Religious institutions are also heavily involved in poor relief and other social service activities that help reduce the tax burden."

Renn cites examples of religious institutions doing great urban work in Indianapolis, where he lived at the time of his essay.

It was Renn's writing that led me to Reverend Tim Keller, founding pastor of Redeemer Presbyterian Church in New York City and author of the best-selling book *The Reason for God*. Keller delivered a plenary speech at an international conference on the future of Christianity in 2010 in Cape Town, and prepared a paper beforehand. It was all about what makes cities tick:

"Today, a city is defined almost exclusively in terms of population size. Larger population centers are called 'cities,' smaller ones 'towns,' and the smallest are 'villages.' We must not impose our current usage on the biblical term, however. The main Hebrew word for city, 'iyr,' means any human settlement surrounded by some fortification or wall. Most ancient cities numbered only about 1,000–3,000 in population. 'City' in the Bible meant not so much population size as density...In a fortified city, the people lived close to one another in tightly compacted houses and streets. In fact, most ancient cities were estimated to be five to ten acres, with 240 residents per acre. By comparison, contemporary Manhattan in New York City houses only 105 residents per acre.

"In ancient times, then, a city was what would today be called a 'mixed use' walkable human settlement. Because of the population's density, there were places to live and work, to buy and sell, to pursue and enjoy art, to worship and to seek justice—all within an easy walk…

"What makes a city a city is proximity. It brings people—and therefore residences, workplaces, and cultural institutions—together. It creates street life and marketplaces, bringing about more person-to-person interactions and exchanges in a day than are possible anywhere else. This is what the Biblical writers meant when they talked about a 'city.'"

Wow. And that's less than three paragraphs of an eight-page essay.

Jerusalem's Old City *(photo courtesy of acroll/Alistair)*

I have never met Keller, but I did watch a recording of one of his talks. A lot of what he has to say is about evangelism, or winning additional converts to his religion. That's not my favorite part of it, I must say. But he evinces an important understanding of what is special about contemporary urban life, including the following:

- Many cultural differences among people, requiring sensitivity;
- A heightened importance of work and career;
- An increased number of "edgy" people, who seek change;
- Artists, who have their own way of experiencing life; and
- The importance of helping the poor, and what he calls "justice and mercy" initiatives.

Because Keller wants the church to succeed, he urges people of faith not to seek to change city dwellers but to embrace the diversity and energy of city life and what makes urbanites different from their rural counterparts. Even those of us who are secular can benefit from Keller's message of diversity, tolerance, and, ultimately, urbanism. For a start, how are we going to improve our communities if we do not try to understand each other? That seems at the heart of Keller's message.

Another religious thinker and scholar, Eric Jacobsen, is senior pastor of First Presbyterian Church in Tacoma, Washington. His 2012 book, *The Space Between: A Christian Engagement with the Built Environment*, which I reviewed for the blog I write for NRDC, makes a very explicit case that people of faith have a special calling to care for cities. Further, Jacobsen believes—and I suspect Keller would agree—that the form of cities matters to the success of faithful practice.

I want to spend some time on *The Space Between* here, because I find its arguments revealing in their understanding of what makes cities work. If I could boil down Jacobsen's theses into a few sentences, they would go something like this:

- Faith is not something you have but something you practice.
- The true practice of faith requires personal interaction with people and place.
- This practice is facilitated by cities, whose form and shape become critical to its success.

The book's title comes from Jacobsen's assertion that, when it comes to the physical form of communities, the spaces between the buildings matter as much as, and often more than, the buildings themselves. I agree. (There is also, of course, a Dave Matthews song of the same name, and a movie, but neither comes up.) He begins by observing that his belief about the importance of cities is not widely shared among Americans of faith, who increasingly see "community" as about relationships detached from particular geographic places. Indeed, the rise of ever-more-sophisticated communications technology and social media are reinforcing concepts of community divorced from place.

In addition, as Jacobsen elaborates later in the book, in the US cities are up against a deep-rooted anti-urban bias that dates back at least to Thomas Jefferson. Cities and the urban form tend to be neglected even by environmentalists, he asserts, because "green ideology is a rural agrarian ideology." (He's increasingly but not entirely wrong about that, in my opinion.) He believes this is mistaken given the relatively smaller environmental footprints of city dwellers, as David Owen's book *Green Metropolis*, which Jacobsen quotes at some length, documents.

Copenhagen *(photo courtesy of Payton Chung)*

Jacobsen believes the Holy Bible is on the side of cities. He notes that the Bible repeatedly describes humans' natural habitat and aspiration (even though beginning in the Garden of Eden) as in and toward cities:

> "In John's vision of the coming reign of Christ, he is given an evocative picture of our lives when our relationship with God is fully restored. And that picture is not of a garden or a wilderness, but of a city."

Among many additional biblical references to cities, he later quotes the prophet Zechariah:

> "Thus says the LORD of hosts: Old men and old women shall again sit in the streets of Jerusalem, each with staff in hand because of their great age. And the streets of the city shall be full of boys and girls playing in its streets."

Central to *The Space Between* is the concept of *shalom*, which we usually translate simply as "peace" but which Jacobsen believes contains much more meaning, including restored fellowship, human flourishing, justice, and "relational wholeness" for everyone. He is not sparing in his measure of newer suburban development against that ideal: Jacobsen argues that, while each one of us carries a longing for *shalom* deep within, much of our recently built human settlement "bears not the slightest hint of that blessed condition that is described in the Bible."

One of the ways in which we fail to move closer to *shalom*, he continues, is that today we experience our world not with our bodies and senses at human speeds, as Jacobsen believes God intended, but through automobiles and a world designed almost wholly to accommodate them. He cites several biblical passages that suggest something quite different, that *walking* is central to observant living.

In his chapter "A Theology of Place," Jacobsen says that "place is an extremely important concept in the Bible," particularly "enacted place[s]," those public spaces that draw people to animate them.

Such spaces may be especially significant to the Christian community because people of faith are called to participate in public life as
witnesses and ambassadors. Gathered worship is an important part
of faithful life, and we should consider how our religious expression
extends to the public realm.

Jacobsen also believes that faith calls us to honor the importance of place with respect to such elusive concepts as legacy, lovability, and beauty. On legacy, for example, he notes that the church in
which he was baptized still stands today, symbolizing that his bap-
tism was not just an isolated act but a continuation of longstanding
culture and tradition. On lovability, he quotes G.K. Chesterton, who
said that the city of Rome did not become loved because it was great
but, rather, that it became great because it was loved. I think I am
with Jacobsen on this.

I was particularly struck by the chapter titled "A Theology of
Beauty," in which Jacobsen notes that the New Revised Standard
Version of the Bible mentions "beauty" or "beautiful" 90 times. I
was pleasantly shocked to see the famous 16th-century Protestant
reformer John Calvin, who even disdained music in his Geneva services and generally is thought of as having been ascetic and severe,
quoted at length on the subject:

> "Now if we ponder to what end God created food, we
> shall find that he meant not only to provide for necessity
> but also for delight and good cheer. Thus the purpose of
> clothing, apart from necessity, was comeliness and decency.
> In grasses, trees, and fruits, apart from their various uses,
> there is beauty of appearance and pleasantness of odor…
> Has the Lord clothed the flowers with the great beauty
> that greets our eyes, the sweetness of smell that is wafted
> upon our nostrils, and yet will it be unlawful for our eyes
> to be affected by that beauty, or our sense of smell by the
> sweetness of that odor?"

I thought I knew my Protestant history, but I had no idea.

Halifax, Nova Scotia *(photo by F. Kaid Benfield)*

Jacobsen even goes so far as to state that "one of the elements that distinguishes Christianity from some of the major Eastern religions (Buddhism, for instance) is its basic affirmation of sensuous desire." (That statement certainly confirms that Jacobsen could not possibly have grown up, as I did, in the church culture of Asheville, North Carolina in the 1960s. As for Eastern religions and sensuality, I would gently suggest that the ancient Hindu text *Kama Sutra* is far more instructive on these matters than anything I learned in my Methodist Youth Fellowship.)

Jacobsen strongly identifies with the new urbanist school of architecture and planning but ultimately concludes that even the best elements of physical urban form cannot in themselves create true community. He contrasts the architectural success but social limitations of the iconic new urbanist development Seaside, in Florida, with the messier but more genuine and organic city of Missoula, where he formerly lived:

> "Missoula has the advantage over Seaside of a permanent community of residents who can use whatever urban

amenities are available as a loom upon which they can weave
the fabric of the community together. And Missoula has
the advantage of having, interspersed throughout the city,
a number of significant churches with active congregations
who help to anchor and give depth to the urban texture...

"To understand these inhibitors to and incubators for
human community, the New Urbanist movement will have
to look beyond its vanguard of architects, builders, and
government workers. New Urbanism will have to begin
to listen to the voices of teachers, psychologists, and, yes,
even pastors if it ever hopes to become more than a market
correction and instead be the long-term cultural project to
which it aspires."

If Keller and Jacobsen both make a strong case that cities are
important to faithful practice, Jacobsen also articulates why he believes that religion is important to cities. Churches play a unique role
in fostering community, Jacobsen argues, because they set a "living
tradition" of predictable and periodic ritual that goes back generations. Even a new church in a new residential area "can tie the neighborhood into a tradition that is thousands of years old and can bring
much-needed depth and perspective into a community. A local congregation can also provide a witness of permanence and connection
among the disparate individuals within a community."

Jacobsen much prefers that, for churches to function well, they
be located in a community's center or at least integrated into their
neighborhoods.

Perhaps the most important part of Jacobsen's writing asserts
that faith requires its adherents to be welcoming of strangers, reeling
off several citations to biblical passages that support his point. (Along
with being a planning *aficionado*, Jacobsen may also have a lawyerly
streak within him.) He believes that our patterns of development
stand in the way, especially with exclusionary zoning and abandonment of the public realm in newer suburbs, which work against relationships even among familiar neighbors "when everyone enters their

homes through the garage door and spends time indoors or in the back yard." Families with kids tend to mitigate this, Jacobsen allows, but it's one more set of barriers for everyone else.

So what about those who are less well off? Justice is an important biblical concept, Jacobsen writes, especially for the poor and most vulnerable members of our society. He quotes Isaiah in what appears to be a prophetic (heh) admonition against exclusionary zoning and sprawl:

> "Ah, you who join house to house, who add field to field,
> until there is room for no one but you, and you are left to
> live alone in the midst of the land!"

As my own writings do, *The Space Between* struggles with the troubling issues of gentrification and displacement as formerly disinvested city neighborhoods revitalize. (See the discussion above in Chapter 5.) Jacobsen makes a critical point when he notes that some of the logic behind the anti-gentrification argument is disturbing in that, extended, it suggests "that we should keep certain neighborhoods dangerous, dirty, and ill maintained" so that property values would not increase and no one of means would choose to live there. He cites some hopeful research to the effect that stagnant neighborhoods that fail to improve are actually less able to retain long-term residents than those that do. Jacobsen doesn't pretend to have all the answers, but does propose that it is important to maintain different types of housing—apartments, townhomes, and single-family homes of various sizes and price points—in a neighborhood in order to achieve a mixed-income outcome. I couldn't agree more.

*The Space Between* concludes with a wonderfully titled chapter, "A Geography of Rest." The idea is that what Jacobsen calls "Sabbath practice" should not be confined to the Sabbath day, and that our human habitats must provide us with "places that invite us to rest and to engage with one other and with the world that surrounds us without demanding that we give something productive in return." These, he argues, are places of *shalom*. Cities must provide them, Jacobsen argues, "to provide a tacit reminder of what is important."

Fulford Harbor, British Columbia *(photo by F. Kaid Benfield)*

Although the thinkers whose views I have discussed in this chapter are Christian, I do not mean to say that linking cities and religion is solely or primarily a Christian issue. I had the honor in 2009 of interviewing Michael Abbaté, author of the book *Gardening Eden* and a city planner as well as religious thinker. In our interview, Abbaté emphasized that caring for the environment—whether it is urban, suburban, rural, or something else—can be a bridge connecting people of different faiths:

> "The faith I know best is Christianity, but Judaism and Islam also share a heritage that reaches back to a personal Creator God who gave us a spiritual reason for caring for the environment. Buddhism and Hinduism, though different in their beliefs about the essence of God, also recognize that humans and the earth are linked in ways more profound than simply our physical needs. One of the points of *Gardening Eden* is that environmental stewardship is not, first and foremost, a political issue; it is a personal and spiritual one."

Religious or not, you have to love that paragraph and, especially, that closing.

So where does all this theology leave us? In my case, I would say that it leaves me hopeful. Knowing there are religious leaders out there preaching the urban gospel as well as the biblical one is encouraging to someone who wants to see cities become mainstream again. It is invigorating to see urbanist concepts examined in a new context. Ours remains a very religious country: three-quarters of Americans identify as Christian and an even stronger majority claim some type of spiritual faith. What people of faith believe, think, and practice is important to our future, and thus to the future of human settlement.

## More about Faith in the City

### The Boston Project Ministries

I met Paul Malkemes in the fall of 2012 while doing some work in a low-income neighborhood in Boston. I was impressed: for Paul and his wife Glenna, helping make their highly urban and distressed neighborhood—and others like it—better and greener was not just something they did as part of their religious practice; it *was* their religious practice.

In particular, the Malkemeses were working under the banner of a faith-based organization they founded, The Boston Project Ministries. The Project's website says it is "a community-based organization in Boston with a passion for seeing renewal in urban neighborhoods," and that is exactly what our team witnessed when we visited. (We were in the Talbot-Norfolk Triangle (TNT) area of Boston's Dorchester district, helping the neighborhood undertake sustainability planning.)

One of the Boston Project's most important undertakings is helping bring a network of pocket parks and other green space into the neighborhood. Its website enthusiastically articulates the goal:

"A multi-site urban garden will transform the TNT neighborhood by creating a walkable route that connects green spaces in the community. Planned play areas, passive parks, urban gardens and orchards are a few of the projects neighbors want to see come to fruition! A multi-site urban garden will:

- Preserve urban green space and provide balance in an area marked by active housing development. TNT has 300 housing units (source: 2000 census), with plans for a potential 100+ additional units in the next 2-4 years.
- Promote physical activity and neighbor interaction. Neighbors of all ages will be able to relax, converse, play and learn in new open, green areas.
- Encourage healthier eating. The community garden will encourage and facilitate eating fresh, local food.
- Provide learning opportunities. Collaborations with urban green space groups and local schools will bring learning opportunities to our neighborhood.
- Engage youth in employment opportunities. Environmentally-focused internships for teens will provide youth opportunities to learn skills to equip them for work in the green economy while furthering the goals of the TNT Green Space Master Plan.

Inspire community pride!"

Elmhurst Park, Boston *(photo by F. Kaid Benfield)*

The organization has a ten-year plan for converting small, publicly owned vacant lots scattered around the neighborhood into green "islands" to be enjoyed by the community. As the site notes, these spaces will benefit not only current residents but also new households, which the neighborhood anticipates as a result of a new transit station opened in late 2012.

We stopped at Elmhurst Park, a new children's park that had been catalyzed by the Boston Project's advocacy. (The Project was fortunate to be joined in that effort by—in addition to other neighborhood, philanthropic, and municipal partners—the Trust for Public Land, which has long had a terrific program for city parks.) Kids had painted expressions of neighborhood pride ("Together we can make a change!") around the park's perimeter.

Impressively, the Boston Project Ministries are administered from the Malkemeses' house near Elmhurst Park. The house itself is significant: Paul, Glenna, and their family live upstairs, but they have made the first floor available as community space. The highlight is a free, pleasant, and safe drop-in center where youth can come and go at their leisure to do homework or enjoy fellowship. Any neighborhood would benefit from this kind of leadership, and I suspect that Keller, Jacobsen, and Abbaté would approve wholeheartedly.

# 23.

# Think Globally, Plan Locally

Marblehead, Massachusetts during Hurricane Sandy *(photo courtesy of Brian Birke)*

Rising temperatures due to global warming bring increased risks of severe storms, flooding, and drought. What can communities do to become more resilient to these hazards? In this essay, co-written with land use planner and attorney Lee Epstein, we explore some of the risks and potential responses.

Over the past 50 years the average global temperature has increased at the fastest rate in recorded history. Scientists say that if current trends continue average US temperatures could be

3 to 9 degrees higher by the end of the twenty-first century. While year-to-year rates of warming have varied and will probably continue to vary, perhaps even including years of apparent leveling or slight decreases, few dispute that the overall trend is significantly upward. This trend can increase the severity of storms by affecting wind patterns and ocean levels and currents.

Tropical storm strength, in particular, is directly related to the water temperature where the storm takes shape. Scientists say that, over the course of the twenty-first century, warmer currents could cause tropical storm wind speeds to increase by as much as 11 percent and associated rainfall to increase by as much as 31 percent. Moreover, the frequency of extreme storm surges could increase as much as tenfold because of warming temperatures, according to a study by the University of Copenhagen. Climatologists say that sea level has risen about ten inches in the twentieth century and could rise an additional two to six feet in the twenty-first under current trends.

It is probably not a coincidence that in the last decade, the hottest on record worldwide, particularly severe storms hit the United States. The worst was undoubtedly Hurricane Katrina in 2005, which killed two thousand people and caused over one hundred billion dollars of direct damage, not counting the tens of billions of dollars required to reinforce the New Orleans levee system following the storm. In 2008, Hurricane Ike—at one point six hundred miles across—hit Galveston, Texas, and killed more than a hundred people. In the fall of 2012, Superstorm Sandy battered, bruised, and killed in community after community in the northeastern US, becoming the largest Atlantic storm on record and second-most-costly storm in US history, killing 285 and damaging property worth seventy-five billion dollars. Nine of the most costly Atlantic hurricanes on record have occurred in the last ten years (the lone exception is 1992's Hurricane Andrew).

Droughts, floods, and serious storms have always been with us, of course, but they tended to be more intermittent and spotty back in the day than now. Scientists say we had best get used to it.

In the wake of Superstorm Sandy, Juliet Eilperin wrote in *The Washington Post*:

"As the Northeast struggles with the aftermath of the massive storm Sandy, many experts say the government for years has underestimated how much of the nation is prone to flooding, given the increasing likelihood of extreme weather because of climate change and the prospect of future sea level rise.

"These experts, who include not only environmentalists but also community planners, insurers and fiscal conservatives, have pressed agencies such as the Federal Emergency Management Agency to rethink the way the government evaluates the risk of floods. Such a change could affect where and how infrastructure is built and make it harder to develop vulnerable areas."

While even the words "climate change" seem to make some contrarians red in the face, people who worry about vulnerability and financial costs must be more realistic, in order to prepare. Eilperin quotes New York governor Andrew Cuomo, who is among the concerned pragmatists:

"Anyone who thinks that there is not a dramatic change in weather patterns is denying reality. We have a new reality, [but] old infrastructures and old systems."

Rainfall totals that were considered 1-in-100-year events in the 1950s through 1970s had become 1-in-60-year events in the 1980s through 2007. Some scientists say that rain events in the Northeast that are now considered 1-in-20-year events will take place every four to six years by the end of this century.

An article posted by Our Amazing Planet on *Skye News* in 2012 quotes a US Geological Survey report as finding that beaches on the east coast have been steadily eroding for 150 years. On average, the beaches in New England and the Mid-Atlantic are losing about 1.6 feet per year.

Hurricane Sandy heads for shore, 2012
*(photo courtesy of Goddard Space Flight Center)*

Even without violent storms, we have a significantly warmer climate and droughts to deal with. Also in 2012, the US experienced its worst drought in over half a century, with a majority of the country classified in moderate-to-severe drought. June 2012 ranked as the third-driest month nationally in 118 years.

This portends numerous adverse effects on cities and people from climate change—and, to complicate matters, effects will vary widely by type and degree of severity in different places. Some of the possibilities include:

- Lower drinking water supplies as reservoirs are challenged by severe drought in some places;
- Additional stormwater volume, and street and private property flooding from more frequent or more severe storms in other places;
- Coastal flooding from storms and sea level rise, and saltwater intrusion into near-coast drinking water sources (Florida is already seeing this in a big way);

- Power outages;
- Allergies, asthma, and new pests and disease vectors (such as mosquitoes bearing new diseases for northern climes), as plant and animal communities migrate and natural habitats change;
- Health effects due to increasing ozone levels, heat stroke, or problems with severe cold;
- Direct effects on infrastructure, including roads, bridges, and utility systems overstressed by weather and temperature.

None of these is great to think about, or even to write—but cities can and should prepare for them, and they can and should seek ways to adapt to the "new reality," as governor Cuomo put it.

The good news, if we can call it that, is that some cities are indeed beginning to get serious about the difficult and politically sensitive issue of resilience to climate change. And they are doing so in a way that makes them stronger and more resilient in other respects as well.

For example, weather-related disasters from 2008–2012 in and around Louisville, Kentucky (four events in Louisville, two in southern Indiana, and eleven elsewhere in Kentucky) have cost the Federal Emergency Management Agency a combined seven hundred million dollars in damage reimbursements and mitigation grants. And that doesn't account for private costs, such as higher insurance premiums or non-insured outlays, increased health care costs, higher utility bills, and higher taxes to pay for local or state government responses. The *Louisville Courier-Journal*'s James Bruggers wrote about the city's response:

> "Whether it's an example of climate change or just temperamental Mother Nature, the evidence of more extreme weather is mounting in Louisville and across the nation. And city officials and business leaders are taking their first steps to prepare for what some scientists predict could be even dodgier consequences ahead.

"That includes identifying some of the weather threats, ramping up the emergency-response system, buying out some residents of flood-prone areas, introducing green infrastructure such as plant-covered roofs, and launching an effort to cool the city by restoring the vastly depleted tree canopy. And a new, long-range planning effort called Vision Louisville will attempt to factor in climate change, city officials said.

"Much of that work is being done without direct reference to global warming. For example, in announcing his tree initiative, Mayor Greg Fischer cited the need to shrink Louisville's 'urban heat island'—the downtown buildings, roads and parking lots that exacerbate hot conditions in the summer. And many of the Metropolitan Sewer District's changes are tied to an agreement with the US Environmental Protection Agency to greatly reduce sewage overflows—while also helping handle anticipated heavier storms."

After Hurricane Katrina, St. Bernard Parish, Louisiana
(*photo courtesy of Infrogmation of New Orleans*)

Unfortunately, not all cities will be able to adapt: coastal cities, in particular—such as those sited on coastal plains, reclaimed lowlands, or on the edge of wetlands—face severe challenges. The more sustainable a city's design and landscape, however, the better it will be able to handle many of these changes.

Some cities may consider expensive and capital-intensive means for adapting to the new climate reality. Constructing huge levees and pumping systems around flood-threatened cities is one such method, although such a technique doesn't work everywhere and is so costly that it is probably unavailable in all but a very few cases, especially in these days of shrinking government budgets.

Louisville is reportedly considering making the tough choice to buy out residences and businesses in some flood-prone places, and perhaps relocate these folks to higher or safer ground. This approach can actually strengthen the community as a whole if the city makes good development choices by, for example, redeveloping abandoned, deteriorating, or underused properties to house the relocated population. Redevelopment would also allow for design strategies that better support emergency access and egress, such as building short blocks and maximizing the number of street intersections; these strategies also support walkability. But it is necessarily a very, very hard and emotional thing to move established neighborhoods and people.

Fortunately, some of the things that make cities more resilient and adaptable are not so expensive and difficult, but still produce multiple community benefits. As suggested in Bruggers's article about Louisville, cities can do a lot with vegetation, for example, starting by planting more trees from among native and adaptive species, and adding green roofs that reduce energy costs for the buildings beneath them while helping infiltrate stormwater before it becomes polluted runoff or floodwater. Cities can also employ additional green infrastructure such as swales and rain gardens, which mimic natural systems by promoting slow infiltration of stormwater, helping meet regulatory standards for clean water while also cooling summer temperatures, bringing more nature into city neighborhoods, and slowing overflows during extreme flood events. Neighborhood vegetable gardens can also play a role, helping absorb rainwater while also providing a source of accessible food during emergencies.

Cities can also reduce their own contribution to warming. Cities can reduce heat signatures (and summer cooling costs), for example, by using light, heat-reflective colors on surfaces. Metropolitan regions can limit the spread of development while conserving nearby farms and forests; this can have beneficial micro-climate effects, provide space for population migration in the future if necessary, protect local water resources, and maintain the supply of local food. Curbing sprawling development patterns also can reduce locally produced greenhouse gas emissions from driving, as can promoting alternatives to driving—walking, transit use, bicycling—even with urban areas.

Finally, energy efficiency and local renewable energy generation both have a role to play. In general, the less burning of fossil fuel and consequent release of carbon dioxide into the atmosphere the better; reducing energy usage and incorporating technologies such as solar and wind power can also help communities become less prone to power grid outages. (There are also salutary jobs-producing effects from energy auditing and retrofitting to increase energy efficiency.)

Ultimately local communities are in the best position to choose their own means of flourishing in a rapidly changing climate. But the time to start is now, before expense or emergency makes change harder.

## More about Resilient Land Use

### How Compact Development Can Mitigate the Impacts of Drought

I'm not naïve enough to claim that the way we have built suburbs and cities over the last several decades is a proximate cause of drought, but sprawling land use can exacerbate its impacts, in at least two ways. First, the large-lot residential development characteristic of sprawl uses significantly more water than do neighborhoods built to a more walkable scale, contributing to water shortages. According to EPA research, for example, in Utah 60 percent of residential water use is for watering lawns and landscaping; households on 0.2-acre lots use only half as much water as those on 0.5-acre lots. In Seattle during peak season, households on 0.15-acre lots use 60 percent less water than those on 0.37-acre lots.

*The Smart Water Report* by Western Resource Advocates provides additional evidence:

> "Another case study from Tucson shows that astounding water savings can be realized if new urban and suburban developments incorporate mixed uses, higher densities, water reuse, and water-efficient Xeriscape landscape design and irrigation practices. In sum, water use resulting from urban sprawl can be reduced by modifications to development densities (e.g., lot sizes), the chosen type of developed landscape, and the source of landscape irrigation water.

> "These findings provide encouraging news for urban planners and water managers: water use efficiency improves through 'smart development.' Municipal zoning ordinances, land development standards, comprehensive plans, and inter-municipal regional plans all play key roles in creating sustainable development and, as a result, more sustainable water use."

The second way in which suburban sprawl exacerbates the impacts of drought is by spreading more pavement around watersheds, sending billions of gallons of rainwater into streams and rivers as polluted runoff, rather than into the soil to replenish groundwater. Again, EPA research is instructive: for a given amount of development, a more compact growth pattern with an average of eight houses per acre reduces runoff by 74 percent compared to sprawling patterns of one house per acre. This is primarily because more compact growth requires less runoff-causing pavement for streets, roads, and parking lots than does sprawl.

By the way, increasing average residential density to, say, eight homes per acre (or a similar community goal) to achieve watershed benefits does not mean that no lots could exceed one-eighth of an acre. An average of eight homes per acre could be achieved through various combinations of multi-family complexes, townhouses, small-lot homes, and large-lot homes. I'm also not judging people who water their lawns or gardens; I water my own, although I'm fortunate for watering purposes to have a small lot. But the more efficient our land use, the more irrigation is possible without damage to water supply, at least in the Northeast where I live. In arid parts of the country, it becomes harder to reconcile household irrigation with sustainability.

Corn crop in drought *(photo courtesy of Tom Woodward)*

A decade ago, my NRDC colleague Deron Lovaas co-authored a report on the subject of runoff and groundwater supplies. A summary released by NRDC with our research partners American Rivers and Smart Growth America points to enormous amounts of water waste from sprawl:

> "In Atlanta, the nation's most rapidly sprawling metropolitan area, recent sprawl development sends an additional 57

billion to 133 billion gallons of polluted runoff into streams and rivers each year. This water would have otherwise filtered through the soil to recharge aquifers and provide underground flows to rivers, streams and lakes."

While sprawl may not cause drought (or other extreme events), and smart growth cannot solve it, strategic use of land is an important part of a resilient response to climate change.

# 24.

# Sustainability Is Where the Heart Is

Broad Branch Market, Washington, DC *(photo by F. Kaid Benfield)*

Environmentalists, for the most part, operate in a world anchored in science: particular species saved or threatened, grams of carbon or nitrogen oxide in the air, levels of pollutants in waterways, vehicle miles traveled, and so on. These are critical, but so are characteristics that cannot be measured. Places that are not just well-performing but also lovable will be the most sustainable.

We all know city places that inspire romance—places that kindle love, if you will. There are the biggies, such as Paris, Rome, and San Francisco. There are historic districts in many cities with narrow and brick or cobbled streets. There are city squares set against dramatic natural views of mountains, desert, or water, or set against dramatic urban views of skylines, majestic buildings, and twinkling lights. There are tucked-away spots with an architecture of intimacy. Most of us have our favorites.

But I submit that almost all of these city places that inspire love, and others that simply inspire, are also lovable themselves. So also are memorable places outside of cities that create comfort or respite. Is this important? Should those of us who care about sustainability also care whether a place is "lovable"? Shouldn't we only care about the resources it consumes and the pollution it generates?

I reject the assumption that great numbers on sustainability indicators make a great place, or that whether a place is great doesn't matter if it shows well on sustainability indicators. In fact, I'll stand these notions on their head and say that places are sustainable *only* if they are also lovable. The truth is that the mushy stuff—legacy, beauty, places that speak to the heart and soul—matters. But what about the whole "it's in the eye of the beholder" thing? If we can't reach consensus on a definition of lovable, then how do we know when we have it?

I'll grant that lovability—or beauty—can be elusive to define, especially over time. For people, being what we now consider overweight and unattractive was once considered a desirable indicator of wealth. I'm told that lots of people hated Victorian architecture before they started loving it.

But being elusive to define with certainty is not the same thing as being unimportant. While there may not be unanimity, there are in fact places that are pretty darn close to being universally loved. And they are the ones most likely to be defended and cared for over time, and thus the most sustainable in a very literal way. We need more of them. Lovability alone may not equate to environmental sustainability; but good environmental performance alone may not equate to literal sustainability.

Seattle *(photo by F. Kaid Benfield)*

I think I've always felt this way intuitively, but I wasn't able to articulate it until I came across the work of an architect and thinker who now is also my friend. Steve Mouzon, whom I have mentioned a number of times in this book, is unabashed in his declaration of why lovable buildings matter:

> "Any serious conversation about sustainable buildings must begin with the issue of Lovability. If a building cannot be loved, then it is likely to be demolished and carted off to the landfill in only a generation or two. All of the embodied energy of its materials is lost (if they are not recycled.) And all of the future energy savings are lost, too. Buildings continue to be demolished for no other reason except that they cannot be loved."

Steve prefers to link sustainability with "lovable" rather than "beautiful," because he acknowledges that there is a cold sort of beauty that can be hard to love, and ultimately it is lovability that will lead to the care and retention of buildings. (There are also places that I find lovable, such as the very funky Watts Towers in Los Angeles, that I would not describe as beautiful.) I'm adding "places" to Steve's axiom with regard to buildings, but I am confident that Steve would agree with my addition.

Steve also believes that, while lovability cannot be precisely defined, there are elements one can draw from classicism that can "stack the deck in our favor" when creating new buildings: time-honored proportions such as the golden mean. I would add that places that are in close harmony with nature also enjoy increased odds for lovability.

Steve begins to approach the influence of nature in one of his more intriguing ideas, that "harmony with the region" may be an indicator of what may be lovable:

> "Simply put, we might love a little clapboard cottage in Beaufort and a stone farmhouse in Tuscany, but putting that clapboard cottage on a Tuscan hillside would look absolutely ridiculous.
>
> "I suspect that much of the mystery of lovable buildings may be embedded somewhere in the harmony with the region. I don't understand it now, but it's one of my top priorities, because we really need to figure this out."

In the region where I grew up, the extensively forested North Carolina mountains, there is a lot of stone and natural wood in the architecture. That is immensely harmonious with the region, in my opinion. It makes sense there in a way that it would not in, say, downtown Chicago or west Texas.

I would also invoke the architecture of Frank Lloyd Wright here: Wright is unpopular with urbanists because he favored a spread-out sort of aesthetic. I get that, but when you see one of his Prairie School buildings with strong horizontal lines and flat roofs actually *on* the flat prairie, it makes sense to me. Similarly, the residence Fallingwater, one of his best known works, fits incredibly well into its natural Pennsylvania setting, cascading architecture nestled within trees above cascading waterfalls. His architecture has a lot of fans—and a lot of staying power—for a reason.

Frank Lloyd Wright's Fallingwater *(photo courtesy of ssinharoy)*

Basically, I agree with Steve that we don't fully understand what makes a place (or a building) lovable. And I would add that mimicking a place that is lovable may not always be a safe answer. But I also agree that the topic is very important. In what possible definition of "sustainability" can a place fit if it is not literally sustained? In order to sustain something, we need to care. And we don't have enough people who will care just because the consumption or pollution numbers argue that they should. We are so much better positioned if they, and we, can also care out of love.

## More about a Lovable Place

### Berlin's Hackesche Höfe

Is it urbanist, or just urban? Or is it just exceptionally pleasant and appealing? East Berlin's Hackesche Höfe represents many of the things we want our city neighborhoods to be—architecturally impressive yet low-key; a place for living, shopping, playing, and visiting; highly walkable and transit-accessible. It is human-scaled with just the right density and building heights to give pedestrians a comforting sense of enclosure, and it is a bit magical, a place of discovery.

Steps away from the Hackescher Markt S-Bahn station, one enters from one of the main streets into a delightful complex of eight interlocking courtyards. Each is intimate and generally invisible from the others, so one passes through the outdoor spaces in much the way one might pass through rooms in a vintage house, each space harmonious with the others, but distinctive, too: The courtyard nearest the entrance from the main street feels commercial, with small shops and cafes; the next one feels more mixed between commercial and residential; the third feels more residential, quieter. Designed by architect August Endell at the beginning of the 20th century, these were live-work places for "middle class and official circles," according to my guidebook when I visited. The courtyards fell into disrepair after World War II and were restored beginning in 1995.

More specifically, the city of Berlin's website describes this remarkable village-in-a-city's continuing connection to history and diversity:

"The concept behind the 1990s restoration of the Höfe was in fact a renaissance of the original 20th century use of the site. The urban mix where the main areas of life, private residential space, work, entertainment and gastronomy could develop jointly in one living space has characterized this area for over a century. Amongst the Höfe's residents before the War were an Expressionist poets' association in 1909: Der Neue Club, a Jewish Girl's Club in 1916, the Imperial Cinema in 1921, a Jewish Student Canteen in 1913, wine merchants and a family department store. Jacob Michael, the Jewish owner of the property before the War, was forced into exile by the Nazis in 1933. Confiscated as a foreign asset it was only finally returned to Jacob's legal heirs in 1993.

"The SMAD (Soviet Military Administration) requisitioned the property in 1945. The building became communally resident-owned in 1951 after a tenants' association opposed the destruction of its original

Jugendstil façade by Endell. Restoration began in 1995 under a consortium including a residents' association, private investors, local authorities, and was carried out by Berlin architects Weiss and Partner."

Hackesche Höfe, Berlin *(photo by F. Kaid Benfield)*

It is a bit of an intentional community, too: after the restoration, the business proprietors and tenants worked out a scheme that requires that all restaurants and shops must be run by their owners. In other words, no chain businesses. A specified mix of uses—apartments, offices, cultural spaces, workshops, and restaurants—must remain, with rents at a variety of price points. Although it's the sort of place that shows up in guidebooks like the one I traveled with in Berlin, it feels calm, not intense, at least on the two days I visited. I hear some of the commercial parts—which are closest to the main street—now house trendy clubs. But the rear courtyards can feel almost like a small town. There is but a single entrance from the main street, through an archway. I loved it.

# 25.

# Sprawl Is Dying.
# Will Smart Growth Be Next?

Haymarket, Virginia, 38 miles west of Washington, DC
*(photo courtesy of Taber Andrew Bain)*

The discipline of thinking and practice that we call "smart growth" has made immense progress in refining notions of urban and metropolitan form to help create more sustainable places. But two decades of experience have taught us that smart growth advocacy also has simultaneously (1) strayed from some of the movement's important early values and (2) failed to keep up with new ideas that have great potential to improve cities. I believe the discipline must adjust its course or risk becoming irrelevant.

In particular, smart growth today has become synonymous with a certain kind of development: dense, mixed-use, urban (whether located in the suburbs or downtown), and decidedly associated with public transit, walking, and bicycling rather than with driving. Those elements have been part of the agenda since the discipline was created in the mid-1990s and, applied the right way in the right places, are very beneficial to our environment, economy, and society.

The movement has enjoyed considerable success. Indeed, cities are back, and back with a momentum to make them more walkable, less sprawling, and less oriented (some would say less hospitable) to driving. Transit usage is up from recent decades. Meanwhile, suburban sprawl is all but dead, severely wounded by changing demographics and lifestyle preferences that are only going to become stronger over time (as discussed in Chapters 9 and 19).

But, when originally conceived, smart growth was about much more than development and transportation reform. It was also about conservation of land; bringing reinvestment to forgotten neighborhoods in a just, equitable way; preservation and adaptation of historic and cultural resources; and enhancement of environmental quality, to name just a few key goals. Many smart growth advocates remain supportive of these original values. But few of them, particularly at the national level that I know best, actually spend much time on them. To the extent that land conservation, equity, historic preservation, and environmental quality are advocated, it is mostly through organizations and coalitions other than those identified with "smart growth."

Should we care? I believe strongly that we should. If this book stands for anything, I hope it stands for an argument that we do the most good for cities, suburbs, and neighborhoods when we follow a holistic path, pursuing packages of solutions that address multiple goals simultaneously while neglecting none. When we focus only on the form of development, we can get into trouble: placing a walkable development on farmland that should be conserved is a bad result for sustainability, not a good one; so is placing urbanist development downtown that fails to do all it should for equity, historic resources, or environmental quality.

In addition, we are now well into the twenty-first century, and many new issues and applications relating to land use—such as green infrastructure, clean energy technology, and urban agriculture—have become part of the urban dialogue. What qualified as bold leadership fifteen or twenty years ago has become mainstream in many places and is, in my opinion, flirting with becoming passé. And it is not sufficient, by itself, to attain true sustainability of place.

## Moving from the Clinical to the Aspirational

I believe that, at least for those of us in the policy world, the smart growth agenda has become a bit formulaic and even clinical. As I discussed in Chapter 24 on lovable places, we focus on the numbers: we tell ourselves and others, for example, that we must increase settlement density, which we measure in dwelling units per acre or the ratio of building floor space to lot space; that we must reduce driving, which we measure by vehicle miles traveled; that we must reduce carbon emissions, which we measure by metric tons. If we're looking at a growth scenario, we may measure these things on a per-capita basis. It's necessary, but it's also a cold aspiration.

Unfortunately, the fact that we are increasing dwelling units per acre, reducing vehicle miles traveled per capita, and reducing tons of carbon emissions compared to sprawl does not mean that we are making great habitat for people. In fact, we now see that one can do exactly these things while making mediocre places without respite, without opportunity, without nourishment. We worship the word "vibrant" as if human beings do not also need solitude, spirituality, safe places for kids to play, nature. Yes, Columbia Heights in Washington, DC has become a revitalized urban neighborhood worth celebrating, if an expensive one. Yes, Bryant Park in New York City is a wonderful public space if you like your parks busy and lively. But high-density urbanism cannot be our only model if we are to create a world that a diverse spectrum of people want to live in.

It is time to focus more on the *quality* of what we are building. What, exactly, is the world we want? We are going to live in it, and so are our aging parents, our growing children, and an increasingly diverse population. Shouldn't that mean that we need a diverse set of strategies? Is it really good enough to produce urban density that reduces carbon emissions but also overwhelms people with its scale, looks mediocre, and, by the way, creates hotspots of environmental impacts? Should we still be applauding? To my eye, that is exactly what has happened in some places, in the name of smart growth.

ACROS Building, Fukuoka, Japan *(photo courtesy of Arun Katiyar)*

Smart growth in Arlington, Virginia *(photo via Google Earth)*

For example, I can think of one major cluster of development that is frequently held up as a smart growth success story. It added some 10,000 workers and residents to its community around a major transit station over a twenty-year period, while maintaining automobile traffic at a reasonable volume. But it's a high-rise canyon without soul. Some of the most visible buildings are downright ugly to my eyes, and I do not believe they will age gracefully. Not one is inspirational, as buildings with living walls are in London and Japan (see photo in this chapter), as Berlin's Sony Center (see photo in Chapter 12) is with its hybrid indoor/outdoor design. Instead, we have concrete or brick boxes. We should be joyful about this?

Care to guess how much public park space was added to serve those additional 10,000 people? Almost none. It's certainly easy to see why developers like this kind of approach: they can build more or less as much density as their market will bear, while not worrying much about things like sensitivity, community character, nature, and legacy, not to mention lovability. But since when have developers' aspirations been sufficient to guide advocates?

Let's create another example, a hypothetical and more positive one. Let's say we think a public square would be a good way to anchor a walkable neighborhood served by good public transit options. Let's not just make a public square that works for pedestrians and call it good enough: let's make it greener. Let's make it of locally sourced, sustainably harvested materials; in places where it rains a lot, let's incorporate green infrastructure to filter stormwater. If there's a fountain—and I love fountains—let's make sure it recycles its water; if there is lighting, let's make it energy efficient. Let's take advantage of opportunities to bring more nature into the neighborhood with plantings of native species.

Fortunately, some wonderful public spaces with green features are being built; but not many are and, to the extent that they are green, they are being built without much attention from advocates for smart growth.

# Building a New Agenda

The new, more aspirational agenda for better people habitat needs to include not just urban development but also (1) some of the smart growth movement's original, but recently neglected, values and (2) new goals and best practices that we have discovered in more recent years. In my opinion, in today's world smart growth shouldn't be considered smart if it doesn't include green buildings and green infrastructure, if it doesn't show respect to our historic buildings and local culture, if it doesn't foster public health, if it isn't equitable, if it doesn't pay more attention to stewardship of the earth. And these are just the more familiar topics that I know best.

My colleagues in the smart growth world do not disagree with me about these things, but I find it disheartening that, after they nod their heads in a meeting, so many of them go right back to work on formulaic urban development and transportation, because that is what they know how to do. That is where we as a movement have placed the overwhelming portion of our emphasis and resources in recent years. Unfortunately, the current, narrow focus leaves out three-quarters of the twenty-first-century sustainability discussion, which is now not only about urban form but also about health, food, water, resilience, local economic development, opportunity, and more.

In addition, we need to recognize that the process of creating a better, more sustainable world—anchored by better, more sustainable places—is as much art as science. Our communities of the future must not only perform well environmentally. They must also contain beauty, warmth, and places of solitude and reflection. They must be significantly more dense than sprawl typically is, but—and this is critical—they must also sometimes forego additional increments of density in order to maintain light, limit noise, provide privacy, and respect a human scale. They must be conducive to engaging the intellect and the spirit.

When we pursue these more aspirational goals, we are out of the realm of smart growth as we currently know it, and into the realm of placemaking. I believe that, in the twenty-first century, advocates for greener, healthier cities should be pursuing a combination of stewardship and placemaking.

Not just smart growth; great placemaking in Paris *(photo by F. Kaid Benfield)*

But, if you still aren't convinced that we must include art as well as science in our agenda, I'll give you a more strategic reason. Those of us who are advocates of smart growth—and I've been one for almost twenty years—may make our case with numbers, but our opponents don't do that, at least not much (in part because the numbers are not on their side). They appeal to emotion: do you really want, they ask the public, to live in or amidst tall buildings? Don't you want a big yard for your kids or dog? Don't you want to keep the flexibility that your car gives you?

Those are not unreasonable questions, and we must not be dismissive of them. To win more friends, we need a better product, one that meets people's needs while allaying their fears, in a setting that is sustainable. This may not always be easy, but I refuse to believe it is impossible. If our vision doesn't aspire not just to good places but to great ones, beautiful ones, lovable ones—places that comfort rather than threaten or overwhelm—we ultimately will lose this argument. And maybe we should.

So, what about "smart growth"? It has had quite a run, a very successful one, and individualized versions of its infill-plus-density-plus-transit formula are absolutely essential to greener, healthier cities. But the formula, standing alone, won't get us there.

We also need conservation and equity, as the founders of the smart growth movement recognized. And, as we have discovered in recent years, we further need moderation, and nature, and restful as well as bustling places. We need local food, and resilience in an uncertain future, and settings conducive to environmental quality and public health. We need leadership that recognizes that the current smart growth formula is at best a partial solution and that only a combination of these elements (and perhaps others) will produce true sustainability. Without critical additions to the agenda, smart growth as we know it may become as passé as sprawl is becoming now.

# Epilogue:

## People Habitat and the Landscape

Frederick County, Maryland *(photo courtesy of Kai Hagen)*

Cities need nature, as I wrote in an earlier essay. But, at least as much, we need a beautiful, thriving, natural, and rural landscape outside of cities. And cities are critical to its protection. I love cities in large part because I love the landscape.

Looking back over these twenty-five essays, I recognize some themes: the identity and character of cities; the sometimes confounding elements of sustainability; the importance of community; the likely evolution of human settlement into the future; how cities connect to our emotions. I didn't so much carefully plan the themes to fit some overall theory, as I have in past books, but chose them intuitively, based on my thinking and writing over the past several years.

In several parts of the book, I alluded to the important function of cities in maintaining wilderness and the rural landscape. To paraphrase my friend Trisha (also mentioned in the Prologue), natural habitat needs strong people habitat, so that people are drawn to our own places, and enjoy but do not permanently infringe upon those extraordinary places where humans remain secondary to other parts of nature. The importance of natural places is recognized eloquently in the federal Wilderness Act of 1964:

> "A wilderness, in contrast with those areas where man and his own works dominate the landscape, is hereby recognized as an area where the earth and community of life are untrammeled by man, where man himself is a visitor who does not remain."

In between true cities and wilderness is the "working landscape" of rural America—farms, forests, fisheries, ranchland, and more—where humans must act as stewards of the land's natural resources. We need our rural landscape and its bounty to be sustained in order to survive harmoniously into the future.

Indeed, North America is blessed with a spectacular landscape. We must be very, very careful how we treat it. Our most beloved national song honors purple mountain majesties, amber waves of grain, and spacious skies above the fruited plain, not strip malls, look-alike subdivisions, and traffic jams. This, more than any other reason, brought me to environmentalism and to caring for cities, as I saw the destruction wrought by the wrong kind of development on my favorite parts of rural and natural America.

No response to the problem is complete unless we attract people once again to cities and walkable places, to human habitat that complements and preserves our natural landscape instead of desecrating it. I wrote earlier in this book that cities need nature, and they do. But nature needs cities, every bit as much.

This is why I place so much emphasis not just on making cities perform well on environmental indicia, but on making them great. Earlier generations fled cities in droves after World War II. We cannot let that happen again. If there are many reasons why this is important, none is stronger for me personally than my conviction that we must respect and nurture our rural landscape outside of cities. If you care about the landscape, you must care about cities.

Having opened this book on a very personal note as I described how I came to appreciate cities, I would like to close it by describing how I came to care about nature and the landscape. In short, it's because of a road.

Mount Mitchell State Park, North Carolina *(photo by F. Kaid Benfield)*

The Blue Ridge Parkway is a 469-mile stretch of immaculately maintained scenic road that stretches southwest from Shenandoah National Park in Virginia to the Great Smoky Mountains National Park in North Carolina, plus some adjoining land and facilities along the way. Part of the US National Park System, the Parkway follows the crest of the Blue Ridge and southern Appalachians all the way. The scenery is spectacular.

Locations along the Parkway are marked with mileposts, leading to a unique vocabulary of place. For example, I grew up in Asheville, whose main access from the Parkway is via US 70, at milepost 382. Craggy Gardens, where I went often for picnics and hikes, is at milepost 367. The turnoff to my very favorite spot in the mountains, Mount Mitchell, is at milepost 355. The scenic route to the house where my parents moved after I went off to school is Ox Creek Road, which approaches the Parkway at milepost 376.

When I was a kid, my mother and father used to keep a picnic basket packed and ready to go, so we could head up to the Parkway for dinner after their work on warm summer nights, to cool off. It was the closest thing to air conditioning that we had. I can't tell you how many times my church's youth group had some event or other at Craggy Gardens, which is also where my father first introduced me to hiking. Going to Mount Mitchell, at 6,684 feet (every kid in Asheville could tell you that number) the highest peak in eastern America, was and remains a special treat.

On and along the Parkway I learned about wildflowers (particularly mountain laurel and rhododendron), waterfalls, trees, minerals, scenic vistas, lightning, fog, tricky driving, and more than a few black bears that I have encountered up-close-and-personal. It was a good place for these lessons, confirms a portion of the official website:

> "Park resources include 600 streams (150 headwaters), 47 Natural Heritage Areas (areas set aside as national, regional or state examples of exemplary natural communities), a variety of slopes and exposures, and possibly 100 different soil types. With an elevation range of 5,700 feet the Parkway provides a home for both southern species at the lower elevations and northern species on the mountaintops.

> "Taking advantage of this diversity are 14 major vegetation types, about 1,600 vascular plant species (50 threatened or endangered), and almost 100 species of non-native plants. More than 130 species of trees grow along the Parkway, about as many as are found in all of Europe. Added to that are estimates of almost 400 species of mosses and nearly 2,000 species of fungi.

"Not to be outdone by the plants, many species of animals make their homes along the Parkway. Seventy-four different mammals, more than 50 salamanders and 35 reptiles can be found on Parkway lands. One hundred fifty-nine species of birds are known to nest here with dozens of others passing through during fall and spring migrations."

I have driven its entire length two or three times, parts of it hundreds of times, stayed on multiple occasions in its lodges and campgrounds, hiked many of its trails (the Appalachian Trail follows roughly the same route, but usually out of sight from the road), and climbed the adjacent peaks. I've even biked a few sections, though I have avoided the major climbs, thank you very much. And I have also done all of the above on and near the Skyline Drive, the 105-mile extension of the Parkway beginning at the southern tip of Shenandoah National Park and running the park's length to the northeast. (The Skyline Drive was built first.)

It may seem quaint in today's environmental climate, when one of our main goals is reducing vehicle use, for me to wax all nostalgic about a road. But it was my extended back yard, and it's hard to imagine having the same feelings for nature and choosing the same career path were the Parkway not such a huge part of life.

On the Parkway's seventy-fifth anniversary in 2010, I caught a story on the National Public Radio website, pointing out that the Parkway was built with the equivalent of federal stimulus money, "when stimulus funding was popular." The National Park Service's site for the road summarizes its history:

"Groundbreaking took place in September 1935 and the work was contracted and completed in sections. By World War II, about one-half of the road was completed and by the 1960s, all but one section was opened to the public. In 1987, the last section was completed around Grandfather Mountain in North Carolina, including the Linn Cove Viaduct at Milepost 304, an environmentally sensitive, award winning bridge."

Blue Ridge Parkway *(photo courtesy of Joe Flood)*

NPR reporter Guy Raz interviewed Anne Mitchell Whisnant, author of the book *Super-Scenic Motorway: A Blue Ridge Parkway History.* Whisnant says that support for great public works in the 1930s kept the project going, but that support doesn't exist these days, when politicians routinely run against the government:

> "Our level of faith in the federal government [as] a doer
> of good for the public is nothing like it was in the '30s. So
> in a lot of ways, you look back and think the '30s was this
> moment in time when things were done that just aren't
> being done anymore. Not just the Parkway, but all kinds of
> projects that serve the public."

Today, by contrast, a certain breed of politician seems to be clamoring to oppose such potentially beneficial public works as high-speed rail, transit tunnels, and other infrastructure, when these projects could provide much-needed employment as well as substantial economic, environmental, and social benefits. In our cities, we once built great parks, public squares, museums, and libraries, with strong public assistance, support, and even pride. Sometimes those things still happen, but frequently the name of the game now is trying to find ways of funding them with private money. Otherwise, we would be committing the evil deed of, you know, daring to spend public money on the public good, an absolute no-no to some.

But I digress. I am so fortunate that the current anti-government sentiment didn't prevail when the Blue Ridge Parkway was built. It may or may not be the country's greatest scenic road; I'll concede that there are other contenders. But this one's *mine*, and it changed my life.

Texas Hill Country *(photo by F. Kaid Benfield)*

Perhaps your favorite landscape is in another part of the country: the Cascade Mountains, say, or the Pacific Coast; the Sonoran desert or the Badlands of South Dakota; the Natchez Trace or the San Juan Mountains; the great ranchland of Steinbeck country in California, or the farmland of Minnesota or Pennsylvania's Amish country; the rocky Maine Coast or the gentle valleys of small farms in the Catskills. If you're like me, you may even have a secret place or two that you would just as soon keep to yourself, before they become popular and turn into something less lovable.

There is no question that our continent has a landscape of abundant beauty if, unfortunately, less than we once had. Our responsibility to this national treasure requires protective public policy and a stronger ethic of conservation and stewardship. But we also need strong and beautiful cities capable of doing their job of attracting people again. We need cities that nurture and support people, while also being kind to the planet. We need cities of distinction and, yes, emotional resonance. In short, we need people habitat that aspires to the same greatness that characterizes the best of our natural habitat. I remain hopeful.

# Bibliography

Alvarez, Lizette, "On Wide Florida Roads, Running for Dear Life";
    *The New York Times*, August 15, 2011.

American Society of Landscape Architects, *Stormwater Case Studies
    by State*; *asla.org*.

Benfield, F. Kaid, Raimi, Matthew D. and Chen, Donald
    D.T., *Once There Were Greenfields: How Urban Sprawl Is
    Undermining America's Environment, Economy and Social Fabric*;
    Natural Resources Defense Council, 1999.

Benfield, Kaid, "Faith-based Environmentalism: An Interview with
    Michael Abbaté"; *NRDC Switchboard*, May 19-20, 2009.

Bernstein, Andrew J., "Student's bike ride earns punishment"; *The
    Saratogian*, May 23, 2009.

Boese, Kent, "Middle Georgia Avenue Getting 'Great Streets'
    Treatment"; *Greater Greater Washington*, June 9, 2010.

Borden, Jeremy, "Georgia Avenue Corridor Residents Grab a Seat
    at the Table to Influence Development"; *The Washington Post*,
    October 16, 2011.

The Boston Project Ministries, Inc., "Vision for a Multi-Site Urban
    Garden"; *tbpm.org*.

Brookings Institution, "About Us—Metropolitan Policy Program";
    *brookings.edu*.

Brown, Ben, "Dream Home for the New Era: Compact, Connected & Mortgage-free?" *PlaceShakers and Newsmakers*, February 27, 2012.

Bruggers, James, "Louisville Starts Efforts to Adapt to Harsher Climes"; *Louisville Courier-Journal*, October 14, 2012.

Burden, Dan, *22 Benefits of Urban Street Trees*, November, 2008; *walkable.org.*

Calthorpe, Peter, *The Next American Metropolis: Ecology, Community, and the American Dream*; Princeton Architectural Press, 1995.

Care2 Causes Editors, "10 Ways Walmart Fails at Sustainability"; *care2.com/causes*, April 17, 2012.

Chabon, "Manhood for Amateurs: The Wilderness of Childhood"; *The New York Review of Books*, July 16, 2009.

City of Dublin, *Bridge Street: District Background*, dublinohiousa.gov, June 4, 2012.

Clark, Lindsay, Holland, Mark, et al., "Healing Cities Working Group"; *The International Journal of Healing and Caring*, September 2010.

Davis, Kim, "Ask More of the Livable City—Ask about the Healing City"; *The Vancouver Sun*, October 16, 2010.

Doyon, Scott, "Pub Shed: Mapping Your Five Minute Stumbling Distance"; *PlaceShakers and Newsmakers*, January 7, 2011.

Doyon, Scott, "Unplug! Accommodating Our Need to Escape Each Other"; *PlaceShakers and Newsmakers*, January 7, 2011.

Eilperin, "Flood Risk Will Rise with Climate Change, Experts Say"; *The Washington Post*, November 1, 2012.

Ewing, Reid, and Cervero, Robert, "Travel and the Built Environment: A Meta-Analysis"; *Journal of the American Planning Association*, Summer 2010 (v. 76, No. 3).

Fisher, Thomas, "The Next Economy and the 'Next Politics'"; *Huffington Post*, February 1, 2012.

Florida, Richard, "How SoHo Can Save the Suburbs"; *The Wall Street Journal*, October 9, 2010.

Florida, Richard, "It's Up to the Cities to Bring America Back"; *Business Insider*, February 3, 2012.

Frazier, Cindy, "From Canyon to Cove: Schools Say 'No' to Walk and Roll"; *Laguna Beach Coastline Pilot*, October 14, 2010.

Garreau, Joel, *Edge City: Life on the New Frontier*; Anchor, 1992.

Glaeser, Edward, *Triumph of the City: How Our Greatest Invention Makes Us Richer, Smarter, Greener, Healthier, and Happier*; Penguin Press, 2011.

Goldberg, David, "Protect, Don't Prosecute, Pedestrians"; *The Washington Post*, August 4, 2011.

Goldberger, Paul, "Neighborhood Watch: Eric Owen Moss and Culver City"; *The New Yorker*, December 20, 2010.

Goodyear, Sarah, "How Cars Destroy the Wilderness of Childhood"; *StreetsBlog Network*, July 29, 2009.

Grocoff, Matt, *greenovationtv: Real Homes + Real Improvement*; *mattgrocoff.com*.

Grow Dat Youth Farm, "Grow Dat Program"; *growdatyouthfarm.org*.

"Hackesche Höfe," *berlin.de*.

Henderson, Susan, "The Dreaded Density Issue"; *PlaceShakers and Newsmakers*, May 31, 2012.

Hernandez, Daniel, quoted in Benfield, Kaid, "Agri-sprawl: 'Farming is the New Golf'"; *NRDC Switchboard*, April 21, 2009.

Hickey, Michael, "In Praise of (Loud, Stinky) Bars"; *Rooflines*, May 24, 2012.

Holland, Mark, "The Eight Pillars of a Sustainable Community"; monograph, HB Lanarc Consultants, *hblanarc.ca*.

Izadi, Elahe, "Huge Rooftop Vegetable Garden Coming to D.C."; *DCentric*, April 15, 2011.

Jacobsen, Eric O., *The Space Between: A Christian Engagement with the Built Environment*; Baker Academic, 2012.

Keely, Louise, et al., *The Shifting Nature of U.S. Housing Demand*; The Demand Institute, May 2012.

Keller, Tim, *What Is God's Global Urban Mission?* (Cape Town 2010 Advance Paper); The Lausanne Movement, May 18, 2010.

Kent, Ethan, "Placemaking as a New Environmentalism: Reinvigorating the Environmental Movement in the 21st Century"; Resources, Project for Public Spaces, April 21, 2011.

Konijnendijk, Cecil C. et al., *Benefits of Urban Parks: A Systematic Review*; International Federation of Parks and Recreation Administration, Copenhagen & Alnarp, January 2013.

Kunkle, Fredrick, "A Community Built On a Shared Need"; *The Washington Post*, October 12, 2008.

Langdon, Philip, "Ohio suburb readies itself for a changing world"; *Better! Cities & Towns*, September 10, 2010.

Layman, Richard, "Gentrification and the 'Hood: Continued"; *Rebuilding Place in the Urban Space*, September 3, 2011

Leyden, Kevin M. et al., "Understanding the Pursuit of Happiness in Ten Major Cities"; *Urban Affairs Review*, November 2011.

Michlig, John, "The Lost Wilderness of Childhood"; *Sprawled Out: The Search for Community In the American Suburb*, July 28, 2009.

Milloy, Courtland, "D.C. Election Didn't Just Unseat Abrasive Mayor Fenty. It was a populist revolt"; *The Washington Post*, September 16, 2010.

Moore, Erika Jacobson, "Revised Dulles Town Center Community Design Heads to Final Vote," *Leesburg Today*, July 7, 2011.

Morrison, Van, "The Beauty of the Days Gone By"; *Down the Road*, Universal, 2002.

Mouzon, Stephen A., "Lovable"; *Original Green: Common-Sense, Plain-Spoken Sustainability*, July 9, 2011.

Mouzon, Stephen A., *The Original Green: Unlocking the Mystery of True Sustainability*; The New Urban Guild Foundation, 2010.

Mouzon, Stephen A., "Walk Appeal"; *Original Green: Common-Sense, Plain-Spoken Sustainability*, July 24, 2012.

Mouzon, Stephen A., "The Wellness Lenses of the Original Green"; *Original Green: Common-Sense, Plain-Spoken Sustainability*, December 20, 2010.

Myrick, Phil, "The Power of Place: A New Dimension for Sustainable Development"; Resources, Project for Public Spaces, April 21, 2011.

National Arbor Day Foundation, "The Value of Trees to a Community"; *arborday.org*.

National Park Service, "Blue Ridge Parkway: Frequently Asked Questions"; *nps.gov/blri*.

National Park Service, "Blue Ridge Parkway: Nature & Science"; *nps.gov/blri.*

National Recreation and Park Association, *Synopsis of 2010 Research Papers: The Key Benefits*; *nrpa.org.*

Nelson, Arthur C., *Reshaping Metropolitan America: Development Trends and Opportunities to 2030*; Island Press, 2013.

Niederhauser, Matthew, "New South China Mall: The Empty Temple of Consumerism"; *Matthew Niederhauser Research,* February 23, 2011.

Nisenson, Lisa, "Density and the Planning Edge"; *Zoning Practice,* American Planning Association, August 2012.

Noblit, Jennifer, "Council Intrigued by Corridor Possibilities"; *Dublin Villager, ThisWeek Community News,* December 16, 2009.

Norris, Nathan, *Smart Growth Schools Report Card,* *smartgrowthschools.org,* August 15, 2009.

NPR Staff, "A Parkway Built When Stimulus Money Was Popular"; National Public Radio, *npr.org,* October 10, 2010.

O'Connell, Jonathan, "D.C.'s Growth is Fueled by 20-somethings. Can the City Grow Up with Them?" *The Washington Post*, May 25, 2012.

Otto, Betsy, Lovaas, Deron, et al., *Paving the Way to Water Shortages: How Sprawl Aggravates Drought*; American Rivers, 2002.

Owen, David, *Green Metropolis*; Riverhead Trade, 2010.

*Pisgah View Community Peace Garden: Your Partners in Grime*; *pisgahviewpeacegarden.com.*

Podmolik, Mary Ellen, "Builder Pitches Net-zero Energy Homes"; *Chicago Tribune,* August 3, 2010.

Prairie Ridge Estates, "What LEED is . . ."; *prairieridgehomes.com.*

Project for Public Spaces, "Luxembourg Gardens"; *pps.org/great_public_spaces.*

Putnam, Robert, *Bowling Alone: The Collapse and Revival of American Community*; Touchstone Books by Simon & Schuster, 2001.

Renn, Aaron, "Religion and the City"; *Sustainable Cities Collective,* November 7, 2010.

Richards, Lynn, *Protecting Water Resources with Higher-Density Development*; US Environmental Protection Agency, 2006.

Rosen, Michael, "Trying to Maintain a Way of Life before It Disappears"; *The Villager*, March 6, 2007.

Rosenthal, Elizabeth, "In German Suburb, Life Goes On Without Cars"; *The New York Times*, May 11, 2009.

Sezak-Blatt, Aiyanna, "Sowing Deeper Seeds"; *Mountain Xpress*, August 3, 2010.

Sherer, Paul M., *The Benefits of Parks: Why America Needs More City Parks and Open Space*; The Trust for Public Land, 2006.

Smith, Ken R. et al. (University of Utah), "Walkability and Body Mass Index"; *American Journal of Preventative Medicine*, September 2008.

Smith, Oliver, *Well-being of Portland Commuters: Untangling the Influences*; Nohad A. Toulan School of Urban Studies and Planning, Portland State University, summarized as "Does Bicycling and Walking to Work Make You Happier?" (Research Poster), 2012.

Speck, Jeff, *Walkable City: How Downtown Can Save America, One Step at a Time*; Farrar, Straus and Giroux, 2012.

Surface Transportation Policy Project, *High Mileage Moms*, 1999.

Texas A&M Transportation Institute, *2012 Annual Urban Mobility Report*.

Transportation for America, *Dangerous by Design 2011: Solving the Epidemic of Preventable Pedestrian Deaths*, 2011.

US Census Bureau, "Families and Living Arrangements"; *census.gov*.

US Environmental Protection Agency, *Greening America's Capitals*; *epa.gov/smartgrowth*.

US Environmental Protection Agency, "Location Efficiency and Housing Type—Boiling it Down to BTUs"; *epa.gov/smartgrowth*.

US Forest Service, "Values of Urban Trees"; A Technical Guide to Urban and Community Forestry, *na.fs.fed.us/spfo/pubs/uf/ techguide/values*.

Victoria Foundation et al., "The Happiness Index: A Summary Report"; *victoriafoundation.bc.ca*, April 2009.

Volk, Laurie, and Zimmerman, Todd, *Confronting the Question of Market Demand for Urban Residential Development*; Fannie Mae Foundation, 2000.

Walmart Corporate, "Sustainability Index"; *corporate.walmart.com/ global-responsibility/environment-sustainability.*

Waters, Wendy, "Can You Have too Much Walkability?" *All About Cities*, November 18, 2010.

Western Resource Advocates, *Smart Water: A Comparative Study of Urban Water Use Across the Southwest*, 2003.

Whitley, David, quoted in Terry, "An Oasis of Green"; *Travel With Terry*, April 30, 2008.

Williamson, June, "Retrofitting for Fecundity"; *BMW Guggenheim Lab/log*, February 29, 2012.

Wilson, Alex, with Navaro, Rachel, "Driving to Green Buildings: The Transportation Energy Intensity of Buildings"; *Environmental Building News*, August 30, 2007.

Wilson, Brian, and Love, Mike, "I Get Around"; performed by The Beach Boys and released as a single on Capitol Records, 1964.

Wilson, Edward O., *Biophilia*; Harvard University Press, 1984.

Wolfe, Charles R., "Rediscovering the Urban Eye of a Child"; *myurbanist*, September 21, 2011.

Wolfe, Charles R., "The Continued Relevance of Reclaiming the Urban Memory"; *myurbanist*, June 25, 2011.

Wolfe, Charles R., "The Role of Children in Defining the Evolving Global Urban Environment"; *TheAtlantic.com*, September 23, 2011.

Zachariah, Holly, "Dublin Putting Hope for Future in Latest Study"; *The Columbus Dispatch*, September 29, 2009.

# Index

# About the Author

**F. Kaid Benfield** is one of the nation's foremost authorities on smart growth, sustainable communities, and green urbanism. He is special counsel for urban solutions at the Natural Resources Defense Council in Washington, DC, where he works on positive, forward-thinking approaches to environmental challenges in the places where Americans live, work, and play. Kaid also teaches regional planning and sustainable development practices at the George Washington University School of Law.

art growth
ED for
national
g smart,
e auspic-
es of the                                                          member
of Smart                                                          g cities,
building                                                          awl. In
2013 Ka                                                          *Future
Cities,* an                                                       online
poll con

Pr                                                               ctor of
sustainal                                                        coordi-
nator. H                                                         n. Prior
to comir                                                         worked
in privat

Ka                                                               requent
articles                                                         *es,* and
NRDC                                                             2001),
*Once Th*                                                        *World*
(America                                                         *munity*
(America                                                         *ing the*
*Revenue*                                                        *ld.com.*
Fo
Follow K